LabSim® Manual

The Lessons Only Experience Can Teach

A+ Operating Systems

TestOut

PEARSON

Custom
Publishing

Printed in the United States of America

10 9 8 7 6 5 4 3 2

ISBN 0-536-29683-9

2006200221

EM

Please visit our web site at *www.pearsoncustom.com*

PEARSON CUSTOM PUBLISHING
75 Arlington Street, Suite 300, Boston, MA 02116
A Pearson Education Company

Contents

0.0
Introduction

0.1.2 CHANGE THE WALLPAPER

Scenario

Your client does not like the current wallpaper or color scheme on her computer and asks you make the changes. Your tasks in this lab are:

- Change the wallpaper to Nature.

- Change the color scheme to Desert.

Steps

Complete the following steps:

1. Right click the desktop and select **Properties.** The following dialog is shown.

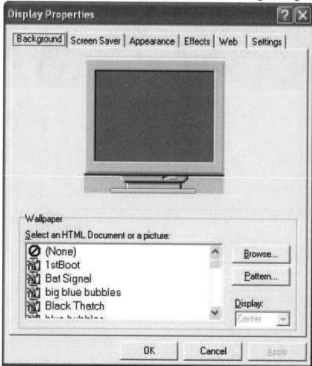

2. Click each of the tabs and examine the possible Display settings.

    Which tab do you select to change the screen area and number of colors your monitor displays?

    _____

    Which tab do you select to use the setting for large icons?

    _____

3. Click the **Background** tab.

4. In the **Wallpaper** list, scroll down and select **Nature**.

5. Click the **Appearance** tab.

6. In the **Scheme** list, select **Desert**.

7. Click **OK** to save the changes.

    Note: In the simulation, your changes will not take effect.

0.1.3 CHANGE THE SCREEN RESOLUTION

Scenario

You are setting up a computer for a client.

Your tasks are:

- Change the screen resolution of the computer to 800 x 600.

- Set the display colors to High color (16 bit).

Steps

Complete the following steps:

1. Right click the desktop and select **Properties**.

2. Click the **Settings** tab. The following dialog is shown.

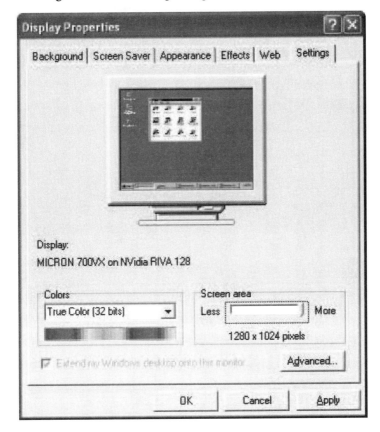

What color settings are available?

_____

_____

3. Select **High Color (16bit)**.

4. Drag the slide bar between Less and More in the **Screen Area** box.

    Why does the window within the screen graphic change in size?

    _____

5. Drag the slide bar in the **Screen Area** until you reach 800 x 600 pixels. Click **OK**.

6. Read the message and click **OK**.

7. Click **OK** and **OK** again.

8. Click **OK** to finish.

0.1.5 SET THE DATE AND TIME FROM THE SYSTEM TRAY

Scenario

You are getting a computer ready for a customer. You have installed the operating system. Now you need to set the system date and time. In this lab, you are required to make the configuration from the clock on the System tray.

Your tasks in this lab are:

- Set the date on your system to October 1, 2001.

- Set the system time to 9:00 AM.

Steps

Complete the following steps:

1. In the bottom right corner of the screen, double-click the time on the System tray. A dialog similar to this one is shown.

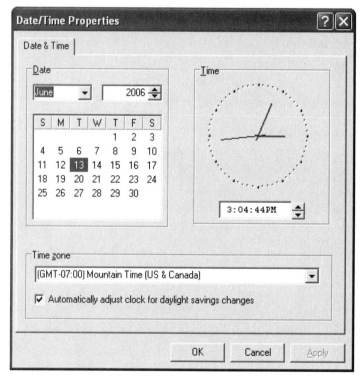

2. Do the following:

   ◦ Select **October** from the list of months.

   ◦ Set the year to **2001**.

   ◦ Select **1** for the day of the month on the calendar.

   ◦ Set the time to **9:00 AM**.

   Click **OK** to apply the changes.

0.1.6 SET THE DATE AND TIME FROM THE CONTROL PANEL

Scenario

You are getting a computer ready for a customer. You have installed the operating system. Now you need to set the system date and time. You are required to make the configuration from the Control Panel.

Your tasks in this lab are:

- Set the date on your system to December 1, 2002.

- Set the system time to 1:00 PM.

Steps

Complete the following steps:

1. Click **Start/Settings/Control Panel**.

2. Double-click the **Date/Time** applet.

3. Do the following:

    ○ Select **December** from the list of months.

    ○ Set the year to **2002**.

    ○ Select **1** for the day of the month on the calendar.

    ○ Set the time to **1:00 PM**.

    Click **OK**.

0.1.7 SET THE DATE AND TIME FROM THE MS-DOS PROMPT

Scenario

You are getting a computer ready for a customer. You have installed the operating system. Now you need to set the system date and time. In this lab, you are required to make the configuration from the MS-DOS prompt.

Your tasks in this lab are:

- Set the date on your system to November 15, 2001.

- Set the system time to 3:34 PM.

Steps

Complete the following steps:

1. Click **Start/Programs/MS-DOS Prompt** to open the following command prompt as shown in the following graphic.

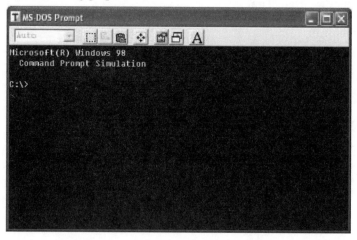

2. At the C:\> prompt, type **date** and press the Enter key.

3. Type the new date using the format mm-dd-yy and press Enter.

4. Type **time** and press Enter.

5. Type the new time using the format hh:mm:ssPM and press Enter.

0.1.8 SET THE DATE AND TIME

Scenario

You are getting a computer ready for a customer. You have installed the operating system. Now you need to set the system date and time.

Your tasks in this lab are:

- Set the date on your system to January 1, 2002.

- Set the system time to 11:00 AM.

Note: You may use any method to set the data and time.

Steps

Complete the following steps:

1. Double click the time in the System tray on the bottom right of the screen to open the Date/Time applet.

2. In the Date/Time applet, do the following:

    ○   Select **January** from the list of months.

    ○   Set the year to **2002**.

    ○   Select **1** for the day of the month on the calendar.

    ○   Set the time to **11:00 AM**.

    Click **OK**.

0.1.10 CREATE A SHORTCUT 1

Scenario

You have a Windows 2000 computer. You are studying the TestOut A+ OS Course and want to create a shortcut to the program on your desktop for easy access.

Your task is:

- From the desktop, create a shortcut on the desktop for CbtEng.exe located in the C:\ Testout folder.

Steps

Complete the following steps:

1. After starting the simulator, review the scenario and click **Continue**.

2. Right-click the desktop and select **New | Shortcut**. The following dialog is shown.

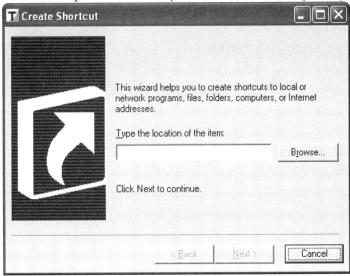

3. Click the **Browse...** button.

4. Double-click the **C:** drive to expand it, then double-click the **TestOut** folder and click **CbtEng.exe**. Click **OK**.

5. Click **Next** to continue.

6. Accept the default shortcut name and click **Finish**.

0.1.11 CREATE A SHORTCUT 2

Scenario

You are working on a Windows 2000 computer. You use a program to view images very often and you want to create a shortcut of the program on your desktop so you can easily access it.

Your task is:

- From the desktop, create a shortcut on the desktop for the ViewImg program located in the C:\Testout folder.

Steps

Complete the following steps:

1. After starting the simulator, review the scenario and click **Continue**.

2. Right-click the desktop and select **New | Shortcut**.

3. Click the **Browse...** button.

4. Expand **C:\TestOut** and select **ViewImg.exe**. Click **OK**.

5. Click **Next** to continue.

6. Accept the default shortcut name and click **Finish**.

0.1.12 DELETE A SHORTCUT

Scenario

You have an Internet Explorer shortcut on your Windows 2000 desktop and do not want it to be on the desktop any more.

Your task in this lab is:

· Delete the Internet Explorer shortcut on the desktop.

Steps

Complete the following steps:

1. After starting the simulator, review the scenario and click **Continue**.

2. Right-click the **Internet Explorer** shortcut and select **Delete**.

   What will happen to the deleted shortcut?

   _____

3. Click **Yes** to confirm the deletion.

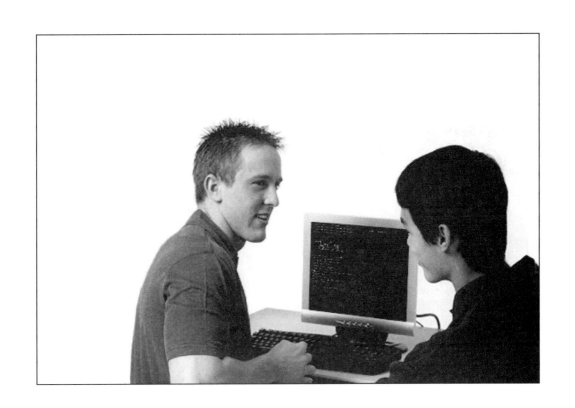

1.0

System Startup

1.1.2 THE WIN98 BOOT PROCESS, PART 1

Scenario

A large corporation has hired you in their computer support department. Specifically, your job is to troubleshoot problems that occur as computers are booting up.

- First, you must familiarize yourself with the boot process and be able to describe it in detail.

- Next, you must learn which potential problems can occur during a boot process and possible solutions to those problems.

- Finally, you will be required to troubleshoot a computer that is malfunctioning during the boot process. To do this, you must identify the error in the boot process and then identify the solution to the problem.

Steps

To complete the simulations in this section, you will work in an interface that looks similar to the following graphic:

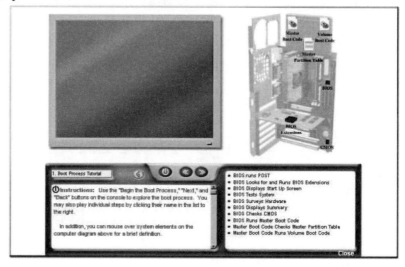

Complete the following steps:

1. Read the scenario and listen to the audio description, then click **OK**.

2. Begin by reviewing the purpose of each boot component. Move your cursor over the parts of the computer on the upper right of the screen. Use the information in the descriptions to fill in the table below:

Component	Function
Master Boot Code	
Volume Boot Code	
Master Partition Table	
BIOS	
BIOS Extensions	

3. To learn how each of these components work together during the boot process, in the lower left side of the screen, click the **Click to Select an Activity** box. Then select **Boot Process Tutorial** from the menu.

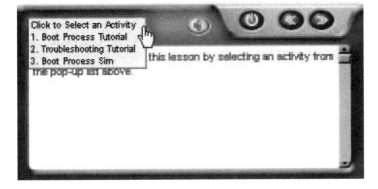

4. Click the **Next** (right) arrow to go to the first step in the process.

    What does POST stand for?

    _____

5. Click Next to step through each step in the boot process and answer the following questions:

During which BIOS step is the master boot code located?

_____

Why does the master boot code examine the master partition table?

_____

6. Now that you have learned about how a normal boot works, you can learn about the different errors that can occur during the process. In the Activity menu, select **Troubleshooting Tutorial**.

7. Select an error in the right pane and use the **Next** arrow to move through the boot process until the error occurs. Repeat the process for each error. Use the information you find to complete the following table:

Error Name	Normal	Error	Indication	Solution
OS not found: Poorly connected hard drive				
OS not found: Faulty hard drive				
OS not found: No valid drive in boot search order				
OS not found: Hard drive not partitioned				
OS not found: Hard drive improperly formatted				
Error loading OS: No active partition				

8. Now that you understand the errors that can occur, it is time to apply what you've learned and to troubleshoot some boot scenarios. In the Activity menu, select **Boot Process Sim**. Six scenarios are randomly presented.

9. Click the **Begin Boot Process** button.

10. Watch the boot process as it progresses on the computer screen in the upper left.

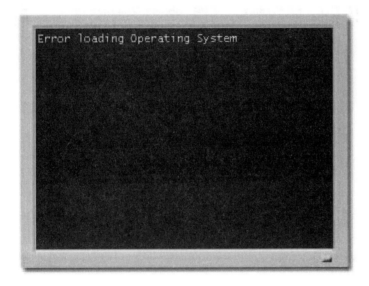

11. In the bottom right pane, select an action to perform on the system as shown in the following graphic:

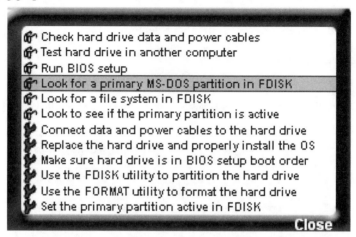

    ◦ Options with the glasses icon will let you determine the status of your system.

    ◦ Options with the wrench icon are possible solutions to remedy the problem.

12. Review the results of your actions in the left pane. Continue trying options and performing actions to diagnose and fix the problem.

13. When you think you have solved the problem, click the **Begin Boot Process** button to reboot and see if the system boots successfully. If necessary, repeat steps 9 through 10 to try additional solutions.

14. After you have resolved the current problem, a new problem will be presented. Repeat steps 9 through 13 until you have worked through each error.

1.1.3 THE WIN98 BOOT PROCESS, PART 2

Scenario

A large corporation has hired you in their computer support department. Specifically, your job is to troubleshoot problems that occur as computers are booting up.

- First, you must familiarize yourself with the boot process and be able to describe it in detail.

- Next, you must learn which potential problems can occur during a boot process and possible solutions to those problems.

- Finally, you will be required to troubleshoot a computer that is malfunctioning during the boot process. To do this, you must identify the error in the boot process and then identify the solution to the problem.

Steps

Complete the following steps:

1. Read the scenario and listen to the audio description, then click **OK**.

2. Begin by reviewing the purpose of each Windows operating system file. Move your cursor over the parts of the computer on the upper right of the screen. Use the information in the descriptions to fill in the table below:

Component	Role
Volume Boot Code	
MSDOS.SYS	
IO.SYS	
Real Mode Drivers	
Registry	
COMMAND.COM	
CONFIG.SYS	
WIN.COM	
AUTOEXEC.BAT	

3. To learn how each of these components work together during the startup process, click the **Click to Select an Activity** box, then select **Boot Process Tutorial** from the menu.

4. Click the **Next** arrow to run each part of the boot process individually.

   What does the MSDOS.SYS file do?

   _____

   How does IO.SYS determine the appropriate hardware profile?

   _____

   Which file processes the AUTOEXEC.BAT file?

   _____

5. Now that you have learned about how a normal operating system load works, you can learn about the different errors that can occur during the process. In the Activity menu, select **Troubleshooting Tutorial**.

6. Select an error in the right pane and use the **Next** arrow to move through the boot process until the error occurs. Repeat the process for each error. Use the information you find to complete the following table:

Error Name	Normal	Error	Indication	Solution
IO.SYS not found				
Non-System Disk or Disk Error				
Error in CONFIG.SYS				
Missing COMMAND. COM				
Bad command or file name				
Registry/Configuration Error				

7. Now that you understand the errors that can occur, it is time to apply what you've learned and to troubleshoot some system startup scenarios. In the Activity menu, select **Boot Process Sim**. Six scenarios are randomly presented.

8. Click the **Begin Boot Process** button.

9. Watch the boot process as it progresses on the computer screen in the upper left.

10. In the bottom right pane, select an action to perform on the system.

    ○   Options with the glasses icon will let you determine the status of your system.

    ○   Options with the wrench icon are possible solutions to remedy the problem.

11. Review the results of your actions in the left pane. Continue trying options and performing actions to diagnose and fix the problem.

12. When you think you have solved the problem, click the **Begin Boot Process** button to reboot and see if the system boots successfully. If necessary, repeat steps 10 through 11 to try additional solutions.

13. After you have resolved the current problem, a new problem will be presented. Repeat steps 8 through 12 until you have worked through each error.

1.1.4 THE WIN98 BOOT PROCESS, PART 3

Scenario

A large corporation has hired you in their computer support department. Specifically, your job is to troubleshoot problems that occur as computers are booting up.

- First, you must familiarize yourself with the boot process and be able to describe it in detail.

- Next, you must learn which potential problems can occur during a boot process and possible solutions to those problems.

- Finally, you will be required to troubleshoot a computer that is malfunctioning during the boot process. To do this, you must identify the error in the boot process and then identify the solution to the problem.

Steps

Complete the following steps:

1. Read the scenario and listen to the audio description, then click **OK**.

2. Begin by reviewing the purpose of each Windows operating system component. Move your cursor over the parts of the computer on the upper right of the screen. Use the information in the descriptions to fill in the table below:

Component	Role
WIN.COM	
Programs	
VMM32.VXD	
Fonts	
Static Virtual Device Drivers	
Dynamic Virtual Device Drivers	
USER	
EXPLORER	
GDI	
KRNL	

3. To learn how each of these components work together during the startup process, click the **Click to Select an Activity** box, then select **Boot Process Tutorial** from the menu.

4. Click the **Next** arrow to run each part of the process individually.

   Why does WIN.COM load both GDI.EXE and GDI32.DLL?

   _____

   Which file determines the settings for the Windows environment?

   _____

5. Now that you have learned about how a normal operating system load works, you can learn about the different errors that can occur during the process. In the Activity menu, select **Troubleshooting Tutorial**.

6. Select an error in the right pane and use the **Next** arrow to move through the boot process until the error occurs. Repeat the process for each error.

    What should you do if you encounter a message that indicates that a virtual device driver is not found?

    _____

7. Now that you understand the errors that can occur, it is time to apply what you've learned and to troubleshoot some system startup scenarios. In the Activity menu, select **Boot Process Sim**. Six scenarios are randomly presented.

8. Click the **Begin Boot Process** button.

9. Watch the boot process as it progresses on the computer screen in the upper left.

10. In the bottom right pane, select an action to perform on the system.

    ○   Options with the glasses icon will let you determine the status of your system.

    ○   Options with the wrench icon are possible solutions to remedy the problem.

11. Review the results of your actions in the left pane. Continue trying options and performing actions to diagnose and fix the problem.

12. When you think you have solved the problem, click the **Begin Boot Process** button to reboot and see if the system boots successfully. If necessary, repeat steps 10 through 11 to try additional solutions.

13. After you have resolved the current problem, a new problem will be presented. Repeat steps 8 through 12 until you have worked through each error.

1.1.5 THE WIN2000 BOOT PROCESS, PART 1

Scenario

A large corporation has hired you in their computer support department. Specifically, your job is to troubleshoot problems that occur as computers are booting up.

- First, you must familiarize yourself with the boot process and be able to describe it in detail.

- Next, you must learn which potential problems can occur during a boot process and possible solutions to those problems.

- Finally, you will be required to troubleshoot a computer that is malfunctioning during the boot process. To do this, you must identify the error in the boot process and then identify the solution to the problem.

Steps

Complete the following steps:

1. Read the scenario and listen to the audio description, then click **OK**.

2. Begin by reviewing the purpose of each Windows operating system component. Move your cursor over the parts of the computer on the upper right of the screen.

3. To learn how each of these components work together during the startup process, click the **Click to Select an Activity** box, then select **Boot Process Tutorial** from the menu.

4. Click the **Next** (right) arrow button to run each part of the boot process individually.

   Where does the BIOS find the location of the master boot code?

   _____

   Where does the volume boot code run from?

   _____

5. Now that you have learned about how a normal operating system load works, you can learn about the different errors that can occur during the process. In the Activity menu, select **Troubleshooting Tutorial**.

6. Select an error in the right pane and use the **Next** arrow to move through the boot process until the error occurs. Repeat the process for each error.

   Use the information you find to complete the following table:

Error Name	Normal	Error	Indication	Solution
OS not found: Poorly connected hard drive				
OS not found: Faulty hard drive				
OS not found: No valid drive in boot search order				
OS not found: Hard drive not partitioned				
OS not found: Hard drive improperly formatted				
Error loading OS: No active partition				

7. Now that you understand the errors that can occur, it is time to apply what you've learned and to troubleshoot some system startup scenarios. In the Activity menu, select **Boot Process Sim**. Six scenarios are randomly presented.

8. Click the **Begin Boot Process** button.

9. Watch the boot process as it progresses on the computer screen in the upper left.

10. In the bottom right pane, select an action to perform on the system.

    ◦ Options with the glasses icon will let you determine the status of your system.

    ◦ Options with the wrench icon are possible solutions to remedy the problem.

11. Review the results of your actions in the left pane. Continue trying options and performing actions to diagnose and fix the problem.

12. When you think you have solved the problem, click the **Begin Boot Process** button to reboot and see if the system boots successfully. If necessary, repeat steps 10 through 11 to try additional solutions.

13. After you have resolved the current problem, a new problem will be presented. Repeat steps 8 through 12 until you have worked through each error.

1.1.6 THE WIN2000 BOOT PROCESS, PART 2

Scenario

A large corporation has hired you in their computer support department. Specifically, your job is to troubleshoot problems that occur as computers are booting up.

- First, you must familiarize yourself with the boot process and be able to describe it in detail.

- Next, you must learn which potential problems can occur during a boot process and possible solutions to those problems.

- Finally, you will be required to troubleshoot a computer that is malfunctioning during the boot process. To do this, you must identify the error in the boot process and then identify the solution to the problem.

Steps

Complete the following steps:

1. Read the scenario and listen to the audio description, then click **OK**.

2. Begin by reviewing the purpose of each Windows operating system component. Move your cursor over the parts of the computer on the upper right of the screen.

   Use the information in the descriptions to fill in the table below:

Component	Function
BOOT.INI	
NTLDR	
NTDETECT.COM	
SYSTEM	
NTOSKRNL.EXE	
HAL.DLL	

3. To learn how each of these components work together during the startup process, click the **Click to Select an Activity** box, then select **Boot Process Tutorial** from the menu.

4. Click the **Next** (right) arrow button to run each part of the boot process individually.

    What does NTLDR do?

    _____

    What is BOOT.INI?

    _____

    What core hardware devices does NTDETECT.COM locate?

    _____

5. Now that you have learned about how a normal operating system load works, you can learn about the different errors that can occur during the process. In the Activity menu, select **Troubleshooting Tutorial**.

6. Select an error in the right pane and use the **Next** arrow to move through the boot process until the error occurs. Repeat the process for each error.

    Use the information you find to complete the following table:

Error Name	Normal	Error	Indication	Solution
Non-system disk				
Missing NTLDR				
Wrong boot				
Non-existent partition				
Inaccessible partition				
Missing NTDETECT. COM				
Booting from C:\ winnt\				
Invalid BOOT.INI				

7. Now that you understand the errors that can occur, it is time to apply what you've learned and to troubleshoot some system startup scenarios. In the Activity menu, select **Boot Process Sim**. Six scenarios are randomly presented.

8. Click the **Begin Boot Process** button.

9. Watch the boot process as it progresses on the computer screen in the upper left.

10. In the bottom right pane, select an action to perform on the system.

    ◦   Options with the glasses icon will let you determine the status of your system.

    ◦   Options with the wrench icon are possible solutions to remedy the problem.

11. Review the results of your actions in the left pane. Continue trying options and performing actions to diagnose and fix the problem.

12. When you think you have solved the problem, click the **Begin Boot Process** button to reboot and see if the system boots successfully. If necessary, repeat steps 10 through 11 to try additional solutions.

13. After you have resolved the current problem, a new problem will be presented. Repeat steps 8 through 12 until you have worked through each error.

1.1.7 THE WIN2000 BOOT PROCESS, PART 3

Scenario

A large corporation has hired you in their computer support department. Specifically, your job is to troubleshoot problems that occur as computers are booting up.

- First, you must familiarize yourself with the boot process and be able to describe it in detail.

- Next, you must learn which potential problems can occur during a boot process and possible solutions to those problems.

- Finally, you will be required to troubleshoot a computer that is malfunctioning during the boot process. To do this, you must identify the error in the boot process and then identify the solution to the problem.

Steps

Complete the following steps:

1. Read the scenario and listen to the audio description, then click **OK**.

2. Begin by reviewing the purpose of each Windows operating system component. Move your cursor over the parts of the computer on the upper right of the screen.

    Use the information in the descriptions to fill in the table below:

Component	Function
Hardware Profiles	
Device Drivers	
Programs	
Registry	
Control Set	
Services	

3. To learn how each of these components work together during the startup process, click the **Click to Select an Activity** box, then select **Boot Process Tutorial** from the menu.

4. Click the **Next** (right) arrow button to run each part of the boot process individually.

   Which file takes control of the boot process from NTLDR?

   _____

   What is a service started by NTOSKRNL.EXE?

   _____

   What is USER32.DLL?

   _____

5. Now that you have learned about how a normal operating system load works, you can learn about the different errors that can occur during the process. In the Activity menu, select **Troubleshooting Tutorial.**

6. Select an error in the right pane and use the Next arrow to move through the boot process until the error occurs. Repeat the process for each error.

   Use the information you find to complete the following table:

Error Name	Normal	Error	Indication	Solution
Service fails to start				
Missing Program				

7. Now that you understand the errors that can occur, it is time to apply what you've learned and to troubleshoot some system startup scenarios. In the Activity menu, select **Boot Process Sim**. Six scenarios are randomly presented.

8. Click the **Begin Boot Process** button.

9. Watch the boot process as it progresses on the computer screen in the upper left.

10. In the bottom right pane, select an action to perform on the system.

    ◦   Options with the glasses icon will let you determine the status of your system.

    ◦   Options with the wrench icon are possible solutions to remedy the problem.

11. Review the results of your actions in the left pane. Continue trying options and performing actions to diagnose and fix the problem.

12. When you think you have solved the problem, click the **Begin Boot Process** button to reboot and see if the system boots successfully. If necessary, repeat steps 10 through 11 to try additional solutions.

13. After you have resolved the current problem, a new problem will be presented. Repeat steps 8 through 12 until you have worked through each error.

1.2.2 EDIT CONFIG.SYS WITH SYSEDIT

Scenario

You want to edit the Config.sys file in your Windows 98 computer. Use Sysedit to add the following commands to Config.sys.

    DEVICE=C:\DOS\HIMEM.SYS

    DOS=HIGH, UMB

    FILES=30

    STACKS=9,256

After you finish the task, save the changes.

Steps

Complete the following steps:

1. Click **Start** and select **Run...** to open the dialog shown here.

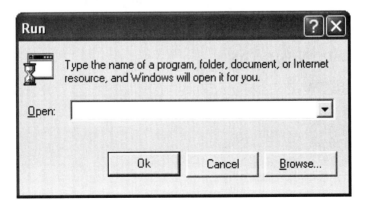

2. Type **sysedit** and click **OK** to open the System Configuration Editor, shown here.

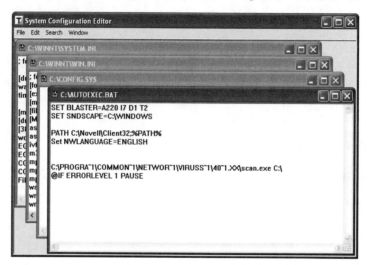

What four files are opened and can be edited in the System Configuration Editor?

_____

_____

3. Select the **C:\Config.sys** window to bring the Config.sys file to the top.

4. Type the following:

DEVICE=C:\DOS\HIMEM.SYS

DOS=HIGH, UMB

FILES=30

STACKS=9, 256

5. On the **File** menu, click **Save**.

1.2.3 EDIT AUTOEXEC.BAT WITH SYSEDIT

Scenario

Your client does not want McAfee's older, DOS-based anti virus software to run automatically on her Windows 98 system when it starts. She has asked you to disable the anti virus software from starting at the system startup.

You task in this lab is:

- Use Sysedit to make necessary modification in Autoexec.bat so that McAfee won't run when the computer starts. If possible, do not delete any information, in case the client changes her mind.

Steps

Complete the following steps:

1. Click **Start** and select **Run...**.

2. Type **sysedit** and click **OK**.

3. In the Autoexec.bat window type **REM** before the following line:

    C:\PROGRA~1\COMMON~1\NETWOR~1\VIRUSS~1\40~1.XX\scan.exe C:\

4. On the File menu, click **Save**.

1.4.1 CREATE AN EMERGENCY REPAIR DISK

Scenario

Create an Emergency Repair Disk. Do not save the registry.

Note: For this lab a disk has already been inserted into the A: drive for you.

Steps

Complete the following steps:

1. After starting the simulator, review the scenario and click **Continue**.

2. Click **Start** and select **Programs/Accessories/System Tools/Backup** to open the following dialog.

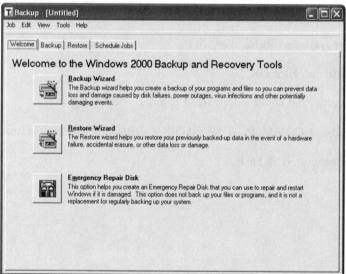

What types of files are not backed up by the Emergency Repair Disk option?

_____

3. Click the **Emergency Repair Disk** button.

4. Click **OK** (there is already a disk in the A: drive).

5. Click **OK** to finish.

1.4.2 CREATE A STARTUP DISK FOR WIN98

Scenario

You want to create a startup disk for your client's Windows 98 computer in case she has problems starting the computer.

Your task in this lab is:

- Create a startup disk with the Add/Remove Programs applet.

Note: You do not need to insert a blank disk into the A: drive for the lab to work.

Steps

Complete the following steps:

1. Click **Start** and select **Settings/Control Panel**.

2. Double-click the **Add/Remove Programs** applet.

3. Click the **Startup Disk** tab. The following dialog is shown.

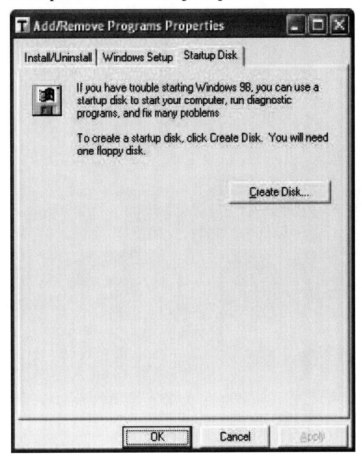

4. Click **Create Disk....**

5. You do not need to insert a disk. Click **OK** to continue.

6. Click **Cancel** to close the Add/Remove Programs applet.

2.0

Managing Disks

2.1.2 CONVERT A DRIVE TO NTFS

Scenario

You are configuring the disks on a computer that multiboots between Windows 98 and Windows XP Professional. The F: drive is currently formatted using FAT32. You want to use NTFS permissions to secure folders on the F: drive. You will no longer let this drive be accessible when the computer is booted to Windows 98. You have backed up the data on the F: drive.

Your task in this simulation is to convert the F: drive to NTFS while preserving the drive's data. The label for the F: drive is Data.

Steps

Use the **Convert.exe** command to convert drives to NTFS without losing the drive's data (you should always keep a current back up just in case). If you format the drive, you will need to restore the data to the drive after formatting.

Complete the following steps:

1. Click **Start** and **Run....**

2. Type **cmd** and click **OK** to open the command prompt window.

3. Type **convert /?** to see a list of options for the command.

    What does the **/V** switch do?

    _____

    What does the **/X** switch do?

    _____

4. Type **convert f: /fs:ntfs**. The following dialog is shown.

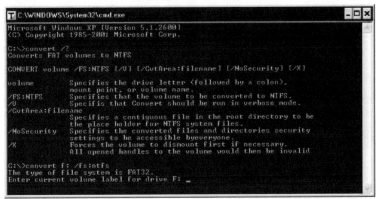

5. You will be prompted to enter the volume label. To find the volume label, click **Start/My Computer**. The volume label will be listed before the drive letter (F:).

6. Return to the command prompt window and type the volume label. Press Enter.

2.1.4 FORMAT A DRIVE 1

Scenario

You are configuring the disks on a computer that multiboots between Windows 98 and Windows XP Professional. The F: drive is currently formatted using NTFS. You want the volume to be accessible when the computer is booted to Windows 98. You have backed up the data on the F: drive.

Your task in this simulation is to format the F: drive with FAT32.

Steps

Complete the following steps:

1. Click **Start**, then right-click **My Computer** and select **Manage**.

2. Under **Storage** select **Disk Management**.

    What is the current file system format for each of the drives?

Drive	File System
C:	
D:	
F:	

3. Right-click the **F:** drive and select **Format...** from the menu.

4. Select **FAT32** as the File System. Click **OK**.

    What happens to existing data on the drive when you format it?

    _____

    What should you do prior to formatting a volume?

    _____

5. Click **OK** to confirm the action.

2.1.5 FORMAT A DRIVE 2

Scenario

You have just partitioned a new computer with one primary partition and one extended partition.

Your task:

- Use the FDISK to check the partition information.

- Format the C: drive.

- Format the D: drive.

Note: You have already booted the computer with a Win98 boot floppy that contains FDISK.EXE and FORMAT.EXE. You can start formatting now.

Steps

Complete the following steps:

1. After starting the simulator, review the scenario and click **Continue**.

2. Type **FDISK** at and press Enter to check the existing partitions.

    What are two reasons why you might want to enable large disk support?

    _____

    _____

    What are two reasons why you would not want to enable large disk support?

    _____

    _____

3. Press Enter to enable large disk support.

4. To display partition information, type **4** and press Enter.

Complete the following table with the current partition information.

Parameter	Value
Number of partitions on the C: drive.	
Size of each partition	
Total disk size	
Primary partition	
Partition type of the second partition	

5. Press **Esc** to return to the FDISK options menu.

6. Press **Esc** again to exit FDISK.

7. To format a drive, type **FORMAT C:** at the prompt and press Enter.

8. Type **Y** and press Enter.

9. Type a volume name and press Enter (in this lab, you can choose any volume name you like).

10. To format the second drive, type **FORMAT D:** and press Enter.

11. Type **Y** and press **Enter**.

12. Type a name you prefer for the volume and press Enter.

13. To check the results of the partitioning and formatting repeat steps 2 through 6.

2.2.2 CREATE PARTITIONS WITH FDISK

Scenario

You have just bought a computer with 8 GB of hard disk space and no operating system installed. You want to get the disk ready for Windows 98 operating system installation.

Your tasks:

1. Partition the hard disk with 40% of the disk space for the primary partition and the other 60% of the disk space for the extended partition.

2. Make the primary partition the active partition.

Note: You have already booted the computer with a Win98 boot floppy that contains FDISK.EXE and can start your partitioning now.

Steps

Complete the following steps:

1. Type **FDISK** and press Enter.

2. Press Enter to enable large disk support.

3. To create a primary partition, make sure that **1** is listed as the choice, then press Enter.

4. Press Enter to create a primary partition.

5. Type **N** and press Enter to not make the primary partition active.

6. To use a specific portion of the hard disk for the new partition, type **40%** and press Enter.

7. Press Esc to continue.

8. To create the logical partition, make sure that **1** is listed as the choice, then press Enter.

9. Type **2** and press Enter.

10. Accept the remaining hard disk space and press Enter to create the partition.

11. Press Esc to continue.

12. Press Enter to accept the logical drive size.

    What drive was just created

    _____

13. Press Esc to continue.

    Based on the warning message at the bottom of the screen, what must you do before disk 1 can be used to start the computer?

    _____

14. Type **2** and press Enter.

15. Type the partition number that will be the active partition and press Enter.

    What indicates that the primary partition is the active partition?

    _____

16. Press Esc to return to the FDISK options menu.

17. Press Esc and Esc to exit FDISK.

2.2.4 FORMAT A PARTITION

Scenario

You have just installed a new hard disk with 8 GB disk space. You want to create a new basic partition with 4 GB drive disk space.

Your task is:

- Create a new primary partition on Disk 2 from the computer management.

- Make it 4000 MB.

- Assign the first available drive to the new partition.

- Label this volume Applications.

- Perform a quick format.

- Format it as FAT32.

Steps

Complete the following steps:

1. After starting the simulator, review the scenario and click **Continue**.

2. Click **Start** and select **Programs/Administrative Tools/Computer Management**.

3. Expand **Storage** and click **Disk Management**.

   How many hard disks are in the system?

   _____

4. Right-click the **Unallocated** space in Disk 2 and select **Create Partition**.

5. Click **Next** to start the wizard.

6. You can only create a single volume type. Click **Next** to continue.

7. Type **4000** for the partition size and click **Next**.

8. Use the default drive letter **H:** and click **Next**.

9. Select the **FAT32** file system from the drop-down list and type the volume label. Select **Perform a Quick Format** and then click **Next**.

10. Click **Finish**.

2.2.7 CREATE AND FORMAT A DISK PARTITION

Scenario

Your task in this simulation is to use Disk Administrator to create a 1 GB partition and format that partition with the FAT file system.

Use Disk Administrator to:

- Create a 1000 MB logical drive in an extended partition on Disk 0.

- Save the changes by selecting Commit Changes Now.

- Format the newly created partition as FAT.

Steps

Complete the following steps:

1. Click **Start** and select **Programs/Administrative Tools (Common)/Disk Administrator**. The following dialog is shown.

   ![Disk Administrator window. Menu bar: Partition, Fault Tolerance, Tools, View, Options, Help. Disk 0 (8056 MB): C: FAT 2047 MB, D: FAT 2047 MB, Free Space 2047 MB, F: NTFS 1914 MB. Disk 1 (4118 MB): Free Space 4118 MB. Disk 2 (4118 MB): Free Space 4118 MB. CD-ROM 0: G:. Legend: Primary partition, Logical drive.]

2. Select the Free Space on Disk 0.

3. Right-click the Free Space on Disk 0 and select **Create...** from the drop-down menu.

4. Type **1000** for the drive size and click **OK**.

5. Right-click the new drive and select **Commit Changes Now...**.

6. Click **Yes** to confirm.

   What should you do after you create a new drive?

   _____

7. Click **OK**.

8. Now you need to format the new drive. Right-click drive E: and select **Format...**. The following dialog is shown:

9.   Click **Start**, then **OK** to continue.

10. Click **OK**. Click **Close to close the Format dialog**.

2.2.9 CREATE A DISK PARTITION

Scenario

You are the administrator of an NT 4 network. The R&D department has asked you to create a new volume for graphic artists to store artwork.

Your task in this simulation is to use Disk Administrator to:

- Create a 1000 MB logical drive in an extended partition on Disk 0.

- Save the changes by selecting Commit Changes Now.

Steps

Complete the following steps:

1. Click **Start** and select **Programs/Administrative Tools (Common)/Disk Administrator**.

2. Select the Free Space on Disk 0.

3. Right-click the Free Space on Disk 0 and select **Create...** from the drop-down menu.

4. Type **1000** for the drive size and click **OK**.

5. Right-click the new drive and select **Commit Changes Now....**

6. Click **Yes** to confirm.

7. Click **OK**.

2.2.10 PARTITION AND FORMAT A DISK

Scenario

You have just bought a computer with 8 GB of hard disk space and no operating system installed. You want to get the disk ready for the Windows 98 operating system installation.

Your tasks:

1. Partition the hard disk with a primary partition.

2. Make the primary partition the active partition with maximum disk space.

3. Format the primary partition and label the volume Win98.

Note: You have already booted the computer with a Win98 boot floppy that contains FDISK.EXE and FORMAT. You can start partitioning the disk now.

Steps

Complete the following steps:

1. After starting the simulator, review the scenario and click **Continue**.

2. Type **fdisk** and press Enter.

3. Press **Enter** to enable large disk support.

4. With **1** selected as the option, press Enter.

5. To create a primary partition, make sure that **1** is entered, then press Enter.

6. Press Enter to make the new partition active.

7. Press Esc to exit FDISK.

8. With the partition created, you need to format the drive. Type **format C:** and press Enter.

9. Type **Y** and press Enter.

10. Press Enter (you can enter a volume label if you wish, but it is not required).

2.2.12 CREATE A VOLUME

Scenario

The manager of the Research department has requested an additional 1000 MB of space on the network. The space is for storing project-related information that must be available to members of the Research department. You've recently installed an additional hard drive (Disk1) in Seattle, and you've upgraded the new drive to a dynamic disk. To fulfill the request, you decide to create a 1000 MB simple volume on Disk1 in Seattle. You are logged on to Seattle in the WestSim.com domain as Administrator.

Your tasks:

- Create a simple volume on Disk1 in Seattle.

- Specify 1000 MB from Disk1 as the size for the new volume

- Assign H: as the drive letter

- Label the new volume Projects

- Format the volume as NTFS using a Quick format

Steps

Complete the following steps:

1. After starting the simulator, review the scenario and click **Continue**.

2. Click **Start** and select to **Programs/Administrative Tools/Computer Management**.

3. Expand **Storage** and select **Disk Management**.

   How many volumes does this system have?

   _____

   How many hard disks does this system have?

   _____

   How much total unallocated space is there on all disks and all volumes?

   _____

4. Right-click the **Unallocated** space on Disk 1 and select **Create Volume…**.

5. Click **Next** to start the wizard.

6. Make sure that **Simple Volume** is selected and click **Next**.

7. Type **1000** in the **For selected disk** box, then click **Next**.

8. Accept the default drive letter and click **Next**.

9. Type a volume label and select the **Perform a Quick Format** check box. Click **Next**.

10. Verify the settings and click **Finish**.

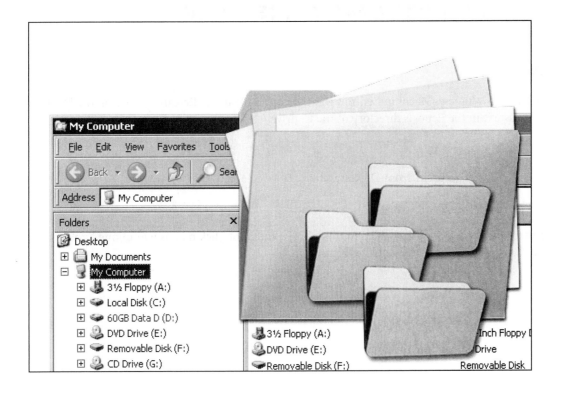

3.0
Managing Files

3.2.1 COPY AND PASTE A FILE

Scenario

You have a Windows 98 computer. You want to copy a file in the Research folder on the D: drive and paste it in the Reports directory of the C: drive.

Your tasks are:

- Copy Research1 from D:\Research

- Paste the file in C:\Reports

Note: Not all methods are enabled in this lab. Use the right-click menus within one Explorer or My Computer window to complete this lab.

Steps

Complete the following steps:

1. On the desktop, right-click **My Computer** and select **Explore**.

2. Double-click the **D:** drive.

3. Double-click the **Research** folder.

4. Right-click the **Research1.txt** file and select **Copy** from the menu.

5. In the left pane, expand the **C:** drive.

6. Right-click on the **Reports** folder and select **Paste**.

3.2.2 MOVE FILES BETWEEN FOLDERS

Scenario

You are working on a Windows 98 computer. You want to move some files from one folder to other on the same drive.

Your tasks are:

- Move Design.rtf and Production.rtf from D:\Process Improvements to D:\Standards

Note: Not all methods are enabled in this lab. Complete this lab within one Explorer or My Computer window. Use either the CTRL-C, CTRL-X, or CTRL-V keys, or the right-click Cut-Copy-Paste methods to complete this lab.

Steps

Complete the following steps:

1. Right-click **My Computer** and select **Explore**.

2. Double-click the **D:** drive.

3. Double-click the **Process Improvements** directory.

4. Press the Ctrl key and click **Design.rtf** and **Production.rtf** to select the files.

   What happens if you use the Shift key instead of the Ctrl key?

   _____

5. Right-click on one of the selected files and select **Cut** from the pop-up menu.

6. Select the **Standards** folder and right click on the Standards folder and select **Paste**.

3.2.3 CREATE A FOLDER

Scenario

You have a Windows 98 computer. You want to create a subdirectory in the Reports directory of the C: drive for research reports.

Your tasks are:

- Create a subdirectory (folder) in C:\Reports

- Name it Research.

Steps

Complete the following steps:

1. Right-click **My Computer** and select **Explore**.

2. Double-click the **C:** drive.

3. Double-click the **Reports** directory.

4. Right-click the empty space in the right pane and select **New | Folder**.

5. Type **Research** for the folder name and press Enter.

3.2.4 MOVE FOLDERS

Scenario

You have a Windows 2000 computer. You want to move a folder from the D: drive to the C: drive.

Your task is:

•   Move the Standards folder from the D: drive to the C: drive.

Note: Not all methods are enabled in this lab. Complete this using the right-click menus within one Explorer or My Computer window.

Steps

Complete the following steps:

1.   Right-click **My Computer** and select **Explore**.

2.   Double-click the **D:** drive.

3.   Right-click the **Standards** folder and select **Cut** from the pop-up menu.

     What is the difference between Cut and Copy?

     _____

4.   In the left pane, click the **Local Disk (C:)** drive.

5.   In the right pane, right-click the empty space and select **Paste**.

     What happened to the **Standards** folder on the **D:** drive?

     _____

3.2.5 COPY AND PASTE FOLDERS

Scenario

You have a Windows 2000 computer. You want to copy a folder from the D: drive to the C: drive.

Your task is

- Copy the Sales folder from D: drive to C: drive.

Note: Not all methods are enabled in this lab. Complete this using the right-click menus within one Explorer or My Computer window.

Steps

Complete the following steps:

1. Right-click **My Computer** and select **Explore**.

2. Double-click the **D:** drive.

3. Right-click the **Sales** folder and select **Copy**.

4. In the left pane, click the **Local Disk (C:)** drive.

5. In the right pane, right-click the empty space and select **Paste**.

   What happened to the **Sales** folder on the **D:** drive?

   _____

3.2.6 DELETE A FOLDER

Scenario

You do not need the Sales folder on the D: drive.

Your task is:

- Delete the Sales folder on the D: drive

Steps

Complete the following steps:

1. After starting the simulator, review the scenario and click **Continue**.

2. Right-click **My Computer** and click **Explore**.

3. Double-click the **D:** drive.

4. Right-click the **Sales** folder and select **Delete**.

   What will happen to the folder when you delete it in this way?

   _____

5. Click **Yes** to confirm the action.

3.2.7 DELETE FILES AND EMPTY THE RECYCLE BIN

Scenario

You are working on a Windows 2000 computer. You have a few graphic files in the research folder on the D drive. You do not need these files any more and want to delete the files.

Your tasks are:

- Delete clouds.png and Backgrnd.png from D:\Research.

- Empty the Recycle Bin from the desktop.

Steps

Complete the following steps:

1. After starting the simulator, review the scenario and click **Continue**.

2. Right-click **My Computer** and select **Explore**.

3. Double-click the **D:** drive.

4. Double-click the **Research** directory.

5. Hold the Shift key and click **clouds.png** and **Background.png**. Press the **Delete** key.

6. Click **Yes** to send the files to the Recycle Bin.

7. Double-click the **Recycle Bin** icon on the desktop.

   What files are currently in the Recycle Bin?

   _____

8. Select **File/Close**.

9. Right-click the Recycle Bin icon and select **Empty Recycle Bin**.

10. Click **Yes** to delete all items.

3.2.8 RESTORE A FILE FROM THE RECYCLE BIN

Scenario

You have just deleted a few files from your Windows 2000 computer and realize that you still need the Employee.doc file. Luckily you haven't emptied the Recycle Bin.

Your task in this lab is:

• Restore the Employee.doc file from the Recycle Bin.

Steps

Complete the following steps:

1. After starting the simulator, review the scenario and click **Continue.**

2. Right-click the **Recycle Bin** on your desktop and select **Open.**

    What is the original path of the **Employee.doc** file?

    _____

3. Right-click the **Employee.doc** file and select **Restore.**

4. To verify that the file was restored, double-click the **My Computer** icon on the desktop.

5. Browse to the location that you recorded in step 2.

3.2.9 RESTORE ALL THE FILES FROM THE RECYCLE BIN

Scenario

You have deleted a few files from your Windows 2000 computer and realize that you still need them. Fortunately those files are still in the Recycle Bin.

Your task in this lab is:

- Select all the files in the Recycle Bin and recover them.

Steps

Complete the following steps:

1. After starting the simulator, review the scenario and click **Continue**.

2. Right-click the **Recycle Bin** on your desktop and select **Open**.

3. Press the Ctrl key and click each file in the Recycle Bin.

4. Right-click the selected files and select **Restore**.

3.3.2 MODIFY FILE ATTRIBUTES

Scenario

You are working on a Windows 98 computer. You want to modify the document that contains development standards for your company. However, this file has been set to Read Only.

Your task is:

- Change the attribute of the file Standard.doc in D:\Standards so that you can modify the file. (Use the right-click menu to open the file properties.)

Steps

Complete the following steps:

1. Right-click **My Computer** and select **Explore**.

2. Double-click the **D:** drive.

3. Double-click the **Standards** directory.

4. Right-click the **Standard.doc** file and choose **Properties** from the menu. The following dialog is shown.

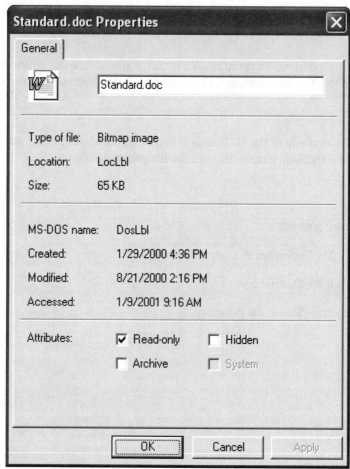

5. Clear the **Read-only** check box. Click **Cancel**.

6. Right-click the **Standard.doc** file and choose **Properties**.

    Why is the Read-only attribute still set?

    _____

7. Clear the **Read-only** check box and click **Apply**, then click **Cancel**.

8. Right-click the **Standard.doc** file and choose **Properties**.

    Why has the Read-only attribute been cleared?

    _____

3.3.4 CREATE A FOLDER AND SET FOLDER ATTRIBUTES

Scenario

You are working on a Windows 2000 computer. You want to create a folder and set the attribute so people won't accidentally delete it.

Your tasks in this lab are:

- Create a new folder in the Reports directory of the C: drive and name it Sales.

- Set the folder attribute to Read Only.

Steps

Complete the following steps:

1. After starting the simulator, review the scenario and click **Continue**.

2. Right-click **My Computer** and select **Explore**.

3. Double-click the **C:** drive.

4. Double-click the **Reports** directory.

5. In the right pane, right-click the empty space and select **New | Folder**.

6. Type **Sales** in the folder name and press Enter.

7. Right-click the **Sales** folder and select **Properties**.

8. Check the **Read-only** box and click **OK**.

3.3.5 SET FILE ATTRIBUTES

Scenario

You are working on a Windows 2000 computer. You have just finished writing two memos and want to set the file attributes to prevent accidental deletion or modification.

Your tasks are:

- Set the attribute of the Memo1.doc file in the Marketing directory of the D: drive to Read Only.

Steps

Complete the following steps:

1. After starting the simulator, review the scenario and click **Continue**.

2. Right-click **My Computer** and select **Explore**.

3. Double-click the **D:** drive.

4. Double-click the **Marketing** directory.

5. Right-click the **Memo1.doc** file and select **Properties** from the menu.

6. Select the **Read-only** check box and click **OK**.

3.3.6 HIDE FILES

Scenario

You are working on a Windows 2000 computer. You have two research files in the Research folder on the D: drive. You want to hide one of these files.

Your tasks are:

- Set the file attributes of Research1.txt in D:\Research to Hidden.

Steps

Complete the following steps:

1. After starting the simulator, review the scenario and click **Continue**.

2. Right-click **My Computer** and select **Explore**.

3. Double-click the **D:** drive.

4. Double-click the **Research** directory.

5. Right-click the **Research1.txt** file and select **Properties**.

6. Check the **Hidden** box and click **OK**.

3.3.7 SHOW FILES

Scenario

You are working on a Windows 2000 computer. You have a financial report file in the Reports folder on the C drive. You want to make this file visible so that you can work on it.

Your tasks are:

- Use Windows Tools to show the hidden files.

- Verify the results by checking C:\Reports folder to see if the file is there.

Steps

Complete the following steps:

1. After starting the simulator, review the scenario and click **Continue**.

2. Right-click **My Computer** and select **Explore**.

3. Double-click the **C:** drive.

4. Double-click the **Reports** directory.

   What files are listed in the **Reports** directory?

   _____

5. From the **Tools** menu, select **Folder Options...**.

6.   Click the **View** tab. The following dialog is shown.

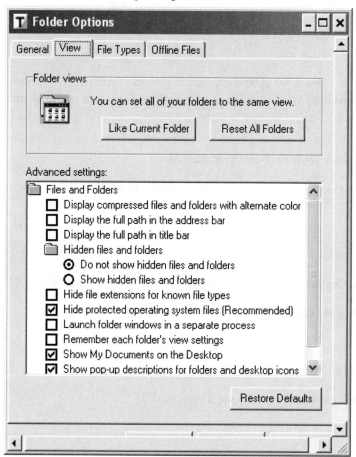

7.   Select **Show hidden files and folders** and click **OK**.

What files are not visible in the **Reports** directory?

_____

3.3.9 CREATE A FILE ASSOCIATION

Scenario

You have just copied the fldropt1.exp file from another computer to yours. Currently there is no file association for .exp files on your computer. You want to edit this new file using Wordpad.

Your tasks are:

- Double-click the fldropt1.exp file to create a new file association for it. The file is located on the C: drive in the TestOut\Aplus directory.

- Ensure that in the future, all .exp files will open with WordPad.

Steps

Complete the following steps:

1. After starting the simulator, review the scenario and click **Continue**.

2. Right-click **My Computer** and select **Explore**.

3. Browse to the **C:\TestOut\Aplus** folder.

4. Double-click the **Fldropt1.exp** file. The following dialog is shown.

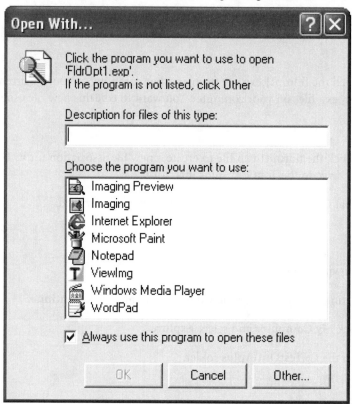

5. Select **WordPad** in the list of programs. Verify that the **Always use this program to open these files** check box is selected. Click **OK**.

3.3.10 CHANGE A FILE ASSOCIATION

Scenario

You are working on a Windows 2000 computer. You have noticed that JPG and PNG image files on your computer are currently associated with the Microsoft Photo Editor program.

Your tasks are:

- Use Folder Options to change file associations for JPG and PNG so that any JPG and PNG graphics will open with the TestOut ImageViewer program (ViewImg).

- Check the graphic files in the My Pictures in My Documents to see if the changes have been implemented.

Steps

Complete the following steps:

1. After starting the simulator, review the scenario and click **Continue**.

2. Right-click **My Computer** and select **Explore**.

3. From the **Tools** menu, select **Folder Options...**.

4. Click the **Files Types** tab. The following dialog is shown.

5. Select **JPG** from the **Registered file types** list.

    What program is currently configured to open JPG files?

    _____

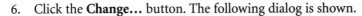

6. Click the **Change...** button. The following dialog is shown.

7. Select **ViewImg** from the list and click **OK**.

8. In the list of registered file types, select **PNG**.

9. Click the **Change...** button.

10. Select **ViewImg** from the list and click **OK**.

11. Click **OK**.

12. To verify the changes have been implemented, expand the **My Documents** folder.

13. Expand the **My Pictures** folder.

14. Double-click a JPG graphic to open it to see if it is opened with ViewImg (verify the icon in the title bar). Click **Close**.

15. Double-click a PNG graphic to open it to see if it is opened with ViewImg. Click **Close**.

3.4.2 COMPRESS A DRIVE

Scenario

You are configuring the file system of a Windows XP Professional computer. You want to provide maximum storage capacity on the computer's D: drive. You decide to compress the drive using NTFS compression.

Your task in this lab is to compress the D: drive and all of its contents.

Steps

Complete the following steps:

1. Click **Start**, then right-click **My Computer** and select **Explore**.

2. Right-click the **D:** drive and choose **Properties**. The following dialog is shown:

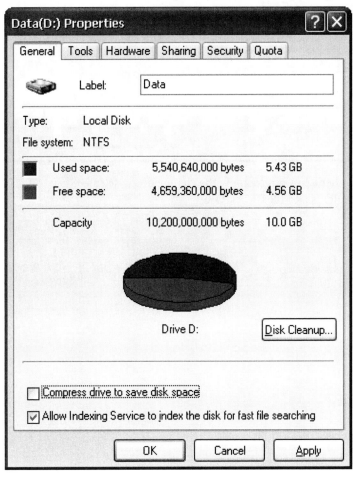

3. On the **General** tab, check the **Compress drive to save disk space** option and click **OK**. The following dialog is shown.

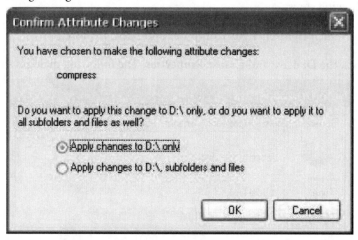

4. Select whether you want to apply the change to the selected drive only, or to the drive and all its subfolders and files. Click **OK**.

3.4.3 COMPRESS A FILE OR FOLDER

Scenario

You are configuring the file system of a Windows XP Professional computer. You anticipate that the Projects folder on the D: drive will eventually store a large amount of data. To save disk space, you want to compress this folder and its contents using NTFS compression.

Your task in this lab is to compress the D:\Projects folder and all of its contents.

Steps

Complete the following steps:

1. Click **Start**, then right-click **My Computer** and select **Explore**.

2. Double-click the **D:** drive.

3. Right-click the **Projects** folder and choose **Properties**.

4.   On the **General** tab, click **Advanced....** The following dialog is shown.

5.   Select the **Compress contents to save disk space** option. Click **OK**.

6.   Click **OK** again. The following dialog is shown.

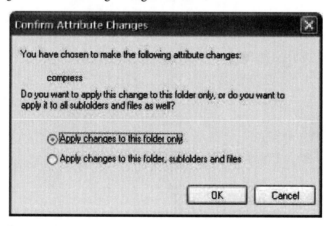

7.   Select whether you want to apply the changes to the selected folder only, or apply the changes to the folder and all its subfolders and files. Click **OK**.

3.4.5 ENCRYPT A FILE OR FOLDER

Scenario

You are configuring the file system of a Windows XP Professional computer. You previously compressed the entire D: drive to provide maximum storage capacity. You now want to show the computer's user how to encrypt the D:\Confidential folder using the Encrypting File System (EFS) supported by NTFS.

Your task in this lab is to encrypt the D:\Confidential folder and all of its contents.

Note: Only the user who encrypts a folder or file (and other users designated as authorized users) can access an encrypted folder or file. Therefore, in the real world, you should let the computer's user perform the encryption.

Steps

Complete the following steps:

1. Click **Start**, then right-click **My Computer** and select **Explore**.

2. Browse to the **D:\Confidential** folder.

3. Right-click the **D:\Confidential** folder and choose **Properties**.

4. On the **General** tab, click **Advanced....**

5. Select the **Compress contents to save disk space** option. Then select the **Encrypt contents to secure data** option.

   Can you set compression and encryption on the folder at the same time?

   _____

   Note: If you were encrypting a file (rather than a folder) and file encryption keys for other users are available on the computer, you can add other authorized users by clicking the Details button and adding or removing authorized users. Otherwise, the Details button will be disabled.

6. Click **OK**.

7. Click **OK** again.

8. Select whether you want to apply the changes to the selected folder only, or apply the changes to the folder and all its subfolders and files. Then click **OK**.

3.5.2 CONFIGURE NTFS PERMISSIONS

Scenario

You are configuring the file system of a Windows XP Professional computer. This computer is a laptop computer shared by multiple users in the company. Currently, all users can view the data on the D:\ drive, but only administrators can change or delete the data. You want to keep these permissions, but also allow members of the Research domain global group to change and delete the contents of the drive.

Your task in this lab is to configure NTFS permissions so that members of the Research domain global group can view and change the contents of the D:\ drive.

Steps

To allow the Research group to perform the necessary actions, grant the group the Allow Modify NTFS permission. This permission includes all other permissions except Full Control.

Complete the following steps:

1. Click **Start**, then right-click **My Computer** and select **Explore**.

2. Right-click the **D:** folder and choose **Properties**.

3. Select the **Security** tab. The following dialog is shown:

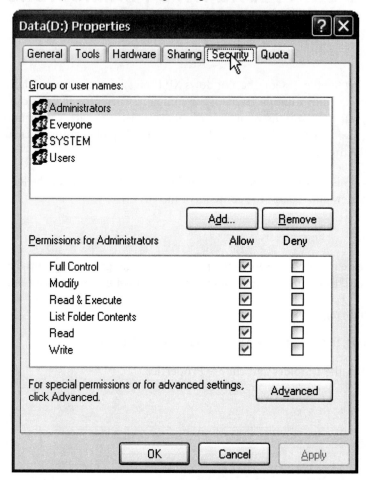

Note: This tab lists each user or group who has permission to the drive, folder, or file. To view permissions for a user or group, select it. The permissions granted to the selected user or group are displayed.

Selecting a user or a group in the top box displays the NTFS permissions in the bottom box. What NTFS permissions have been assigned to the following groups?

Group	NTFS Permissions
Administrators	
Everyone	
Users	

4. To add permission for a user or group click **Add....** The following dialog is shown.

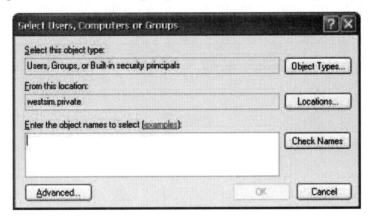

5. **Note:** On the live system, you would be able to type the name of a user or a group. In the simulation, click **Advanced...** and **Find Now** to view the list of users and groups.

6. Select **Research** from the list and click **OK**. Click **OK** again to add the group to the Access Control List (ACL).

7. Select the group you just added.

    What permissions does the Research group have by default?

    _____

8. Check the **Modify** permission in the **Allow** column.

    Note: Normally, you should not use check boxes in the Deny column. Explicitly denying permissions overrides permissions otherwise allowed through group membership.

    What other permissions are granted when you grant the **Modify** permission?

    _____

9. Click **OK** to save the changes.

3.6.2 PERFORM A DIFFERENTIAL BACKUP

Scenario

You want to set up an automatic backup for your computer. You decide to use the differential method to back up the Market folder on the D: drive every day.

Your tasks in this lab are:

- Back up the Market folder on the D: drive with the differential backup method starting at 10:00 pm daily.

- Store the backups on the Travan tape drive.

- Enter your password (study).

- Make sure that the data is verified after the backup.

- Name the backup job MarketBU.

Steps

Complete the following steps:

1. After starting the simulator, review the scenario and click **Continue**.

2. Select **Start/Programs/Accessories/System Tools/Backup** to open the Windows 2000 Backup utility.

3. Select **Backup Wizard**.

4. Click **Next** to begin.

5. Select **Back up selected files, drives, or network data**, then click **Next**.

6. In the left pane, expand **My Computer**. Browse to **D:\Market**. Check the box in front of the **Market** folder. When you are finished, the dialog should resemble the following:

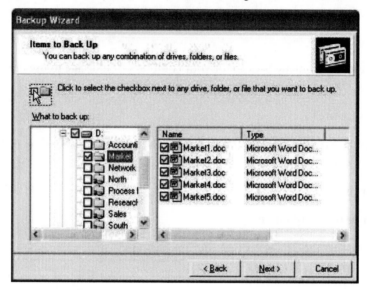

Why is a checkmark placed automatically next to the D: drive? Why is it different than the check mark next to the Market folder?

_____

_____

Click **Next** to continue.

7. Accept the default backup location and click **Next**.

8. To configure additional backup options, click the **Advanced...** button.

9. Select **Differential** as the type of backup to perform, then click **Next**.

10. Select **Verify data after backup** and click **Next**.

11. For the Media Options step, accept the defaults and click **Next**.

12. For the Backup Label step, accept the default backup label and click **Next**.

13. Select **Later** to schedule the backup to run at another time.

14. Type **study** for the password. Confirm the password and click **OK**.

15. In the **Job name** box, type **MarketBU**. Click the **Set Schedule…** button. The following dialog is shown:

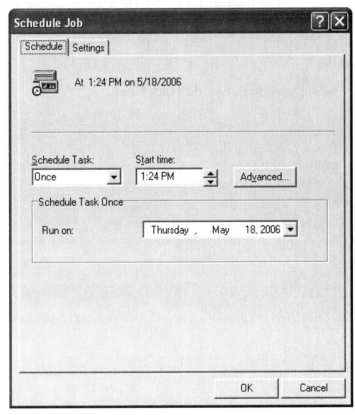

16. Configure the following values:

    ◦ For the **Schedule Task**, select **Daily**.

    ◦ For the **Start time**, configure **10:00 PM**.

    ◦ For the **Schedule Task Daily**, accept the default to run the backup once a day.

    Click **OK** to save the schedule settings.

17. Click **Next**.

18. Review the backup job information, then click **Finish**.

3.6.3 PERFORM AN INCREMENTAL BACKUP

Scenario

You decide to use the incremental backup method to back up the Reports folder on the C: drive.

Your tasks in this lab are:

- Back up the Reports folder on the C: drive.

- Save the backup file to the Travan tape

- Schedule a daily Incremental backup starting at 8:00 pm.

- Enter your password: study.

- Name the backup job: ReportsBU.

- Make sure that the data is verified after the backup.

Steps

Complete the following steps:

1. After starting the simulator, review the scenario and click **Continue**.

2. Select **Start/Programs/Accessories/System Tools/Backup** to open the Windows 2000 Backup utility.

3. Select **Backup Wizard**.

4. Click **Next** to begin.

5. Select **Back up selected files, drives, or network data**, then click **Next**.

6. In the left pane, expand **My Computer**. Browse to **C:\Reports**. Check the box in front of the **Reports** folder. Click **Next** to continue.

7. Accept the default backup location and click **Next**.

8. To configure additional backup options, click the **Advanced...** button.

9. Select each entry in the backup type list and read the description for the selected backup type. Complete the following table.

Backup Type	Backs Up
	Backs up files that have not been backed up Backs up files that have changed Does not mark files as being backed up
	Backs up files that have not been backed up Backs up files that have changed Marks files as being backed up
	Backs up all files Marks files as being backed up
	Backs up all files Does not mark files as being backed up
	Backs up files that have changed today Does not mark files as being backed up

10. Select **Incremental** as the type of backup to perform, then click **Next**.

11. Select **Verify data after backup** and click **Next**.

12. For the Media Options step, accept the defaults and click **Next**.

13. For the Backup Label step, accept the default backup label and click **Next**.

14. Select **Later** to schedule the backup to run at another time.

15. Type **study** for the password. Confirm the password and click **OK**.

16. In the **Job name** box, type **ReportsBU**. Click the **Set Schedule...** button.

17. Configure the following values:

    ○ For the **Schedule Task**, select **Daily**.

    ○ For the **Start time**, configure **8:00 PM**.

    ○ For the **Schedule Task Daily**, accept the default to run the backup once a day.

    Click **OK** to save the schedule settings.

18. Click **Next**.

19. Review the backup job information, then click **Finish**.

3.6.4 USE AN APPROPRIATE METHOD TO BACK UP FILES

Scenario

The Research department has been working on some important projects and has asked you to back up the Projects folder every evening. You know that the developers sometimes come back to work in the evening, so the backup should not take too long to complete. Also you want to minimize the backup storage space.

You have limited the backup media space and decided to back up only those files that are marked for backup.

Your tasks in this lab are:

- Select a backup method that meets your need.

- Create a schedule to back up the Projects folder on the R: drive at 10:00 pm daily.

- Store the backups on a Travan tape.

- Make sure to verify the data after the backup.

- Name the backup job: ProjectsBU.

- Enter a password of your choice when the password is required.

Steps

Before completing this lab, answer the following questions:

Which files should your backup strategy back up?

O   All selected files

O   All selected files that have not yet been backed up

Should your backup strategy mark files as having been backed up?

O   Yes

O   No

Which backup type should you choose?

O   Normal

O   Copy

O   Incremental

O   Differential

O   Daily

Complete the following steps:

1.   After starting the simulator, review the scenario and click **Continue.**

2.   Select **Start/Programs/Accessories/System Tools/Backup** to open the Windows 2000 Backup utility.

3.   Select **Backup Wizard.**

4.   Click **Next** to begin.

5.   Select **Back up selected files, drives, or network data**, then click **Next.**

6.   In the left pane, expand **My Computer**. Browse to **R:\Projects**. Check the box in front of the **Projects** folder. Click **Next** to continue.

7.   Accept the default backup location and click **Next.**

8.   To configure additional backup options, click the **Advanced...** button.

9.   Select the backup type. Click **Next.**

10. Select **Verify data after backup** and click **Next.**

11. For the Media Options step, accept the defaults and click **Next.**

12. For the Backup Label step, accept the default backup label and click **Next**.

13. Select **Later** to schedule the backup to run at another time.

14. Enter a password of your choice, confirm it, then click **OK**.

15. In the **Job name** box, type **ProjectsBU**. Click the **Set Schedule...** button.

16. Configure the following values:

    ◦ For the **Schedule Task**, select **Daily**.

    ◦ For the **Start time**, configure **8:00 PM**.

    ◦ For the **Schedule Task Daily**, accept the default to run the backup once a day.

    Click **OK** to save the schedule settings.

17. Click **Next**.

18. Review the backup job information, then click **Finish**.

3.6.5 USE AN APPROPRIATE METHOD TO BACK UP FILES TO A LOCAL DRIVE

Scenario

Fred, the accountant of your company, asks you to back up the Accounting folder on the D: drive on his Windows 2000 computer to the following location on the network: R:\Accounting\backup\. He wants the backup to be performed automatically every day. He also wants the backup files to save space but also be easy to restore if he needs to restore files.

Your tasks in this lab are:

- Select a backup method to back up all the files in the Accounting folder on the D: drive.

- Schedule the backup starting time at 8:00 pm, daily.

- Store the backups on the network at the following location:R:\Accounting\backup\

- Name the backup file the Account.bkf

- Name the Job name: Fred_files.

- Enter a password of your choice.

- Make sure the data is verified after backup.

- Make sure to append this backup to the media.

Steps

Before completing this lab, answer the following questions:

> Which files should your backup strategy back up?
>
> ○   All selected files
>
> ○   All selected files that have not yet been backed up
>
> Should your backup strategy mark files as having been backed up?
>
> ○   Yes
>
> ○   No
>
> Which backup type should you choose?
>
> ○   Normal
>
> ○   Copy
>
> ○   Incremental
>
> ○   Differential
>
> ○   Daily

Complete the following steps:

1. After starting the simulator, review the scenario and click **Continue**.

2. Select **Start/Programs/Accessories/System Tools/Backup** to open the Windows 2000 Backup utility.

3. Select **Backup Wizard**.

4. Click **Next** to begin.

5. Select **Back up selected files, drives, or network data**, then click **Next**.

6. In the left pane, expand **My Computer**. Browse to **D:\Accounting**. Check the box in front of the **Accounting** folder. Click **Next** to continue.

7. For the **Backup media type**, select **File**. Click the **Browse...** button to configure the backup location. The following dialog is shown.

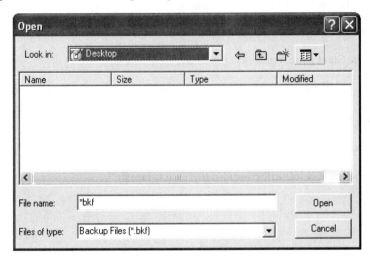

8. In the **Look in:** box, select **R:\\Dev_SRV1**.

9. Double-click the **Accounting** folder, then double-click the **Backup** folder.

10. Make sure that **Account.bkf** is listed in the **File name** box, then click **Open**.

11. Click **Next** to continue.

12. To configure additional backup options, click the **Advanced...** button.

13. Select the backup type. Click **Next**.

14. Select **Verify data after backup** and click **Next**.

15. For the Media Options step, accept the defaults and click **Next**.

16. For the Backup Label step, accept the default backup label and click **Next**.

17. Select **Later** to schedule the backup to run at another time.

18. Enter a password of your choice, confirm it, then click **OK**.

19. In the **Job name** box, type **Fred_files**. Click the **Set Schedule...** button.

20. Configure the following values:

    ◦   For the **Schedule Task**, select **Daily**.

    ◦   For the **Start time**, configure **8:00 PM**.

    ◦   For the **Schedule Task Daily**, accept the default to run the backup once a day.

    Click **OK** to save the schedule settings.

21. Click **Next**.

22. Review the backup job information, then click **Finish**.

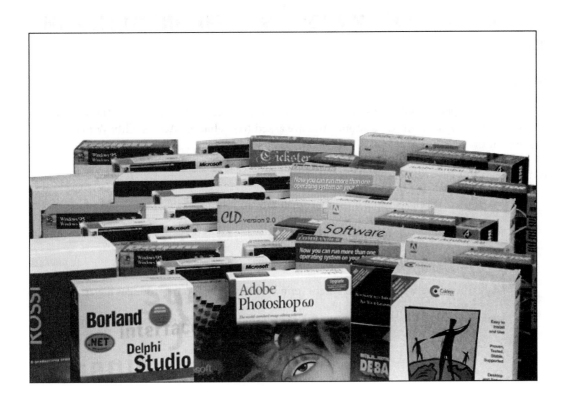

4.0

Software

4.1.2 ADD A WINDOWS COMPONENT IN WIN 98

Scenario

A client needs a special tool to aid him when he is using the computer. He wants the screen to flash when the system makes a sound. You are asked to enable the Accessibility Windows component on his computer.

Your tasks in this lab are:

- Install Accessibility Options using Add/Remove Programs.

- Run Accessibility Options.

- Enable the SoundSentry option.

- Make the active window flash whenever a windowed program produces a warning sound.

- Make the border flash whenever a full screen text program produces a warning sound.

Steps

Complete the following steps:

1. Click **Start/Settings/Control Panel**.

2. Double-click the **Add/Remove Programs** applet.

3. Select the **Windows Setup** tab. The following dialog is shown:

4. Check the box next to **Accessibility**. Click the **Details** button.

5. Select each component and read the description.

    Which component installs the Magnifier?

    _____

    Which component installs options to customize the keyboard?

    _____

6. Click **OK** to close the option details.

7. Click **OK** to install Accessibility Options.

8. Read the message and click **OK**.

9. To configure Accessibility settings, double-click the **Accessibility Options** applet.

10. Select the **Sound** tab. The following dialog is shown.

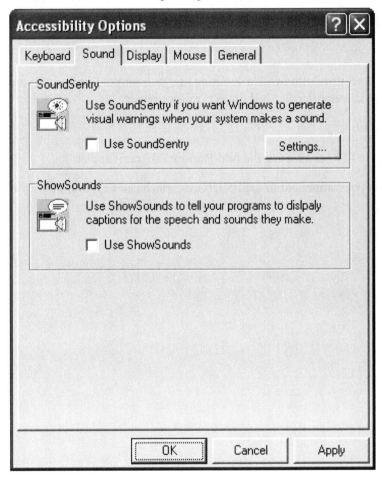

11. Select **Use SoundSentry**. Click the **Settings...** button.

12. Configure the visual warning signals to meet the scenario requirements. Click **OK**.

13. Click **OK** to make the changes.

4.1.3 ADD A WINDOWS COMPONENT IN WIN 2000

Scenario

You have a few developers who work at a remote site. You want to install a FTP server on your computer so they can transfer finished projects to your server.

Your task in this lab is:

- Install the FTP server using the Add/Remove Programs applet.

Note: FTP server is a component in the IIS services, which can be found under the Windows Components.

Steps

Complete the following steps:

1. After starting the simulator, review the scenario and click **Continue**.

2. Click **Start/Settings/Control Panel**.

3. Double-click **Add/Remove Programs**.

4. On the left side, click **Add/Remove Windows Components**. The following dialog is shown.

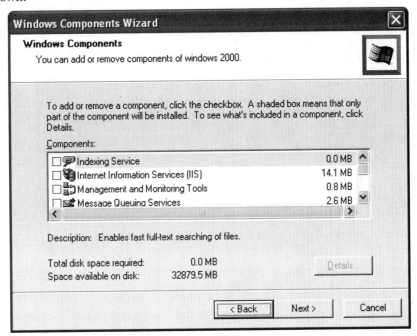

5. Select **Internet Information Services (IIS)** from the Windows Components list. Do not check the box next to the IIS component, as this will install all IIS components (you only want to install the FTP component). Click the **Details...** button.

The following dialog is shown:

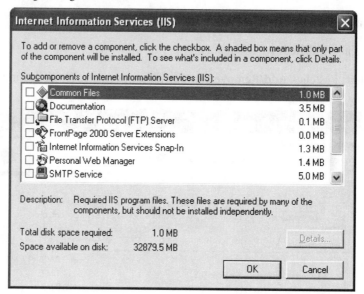

6. Select each component and read the description.

Which component adds support for making Web sites available?

_____

_____

Which component adds application development support?

_____

_____

7. Check the **File Transfer Protocol (FTP) Server** box and click **OK**.

8. Click **Next** to install the component.

9. Click **Finish,** then **Close.**

4.2.1 REMOVE A GAME FROM A WIN2000 COMPUTER

Scenario

You have a computer game named Riven on a Windows 2000 computer. You need more disk space and decide to remove the program from your computer.

Your task in this lab is:

Use the Add/Remove Programs applet to remove Riven from the Windows 2000 computer.

Steps

Complete the following steps:

1. After starting the simulator, review the scenario and click **Continue**.

2. Click **Start/Settings/Control Panel**.

3. Double-click **Add/Remove Programs**.

4. Browse through the installed software list and select **Riven**. Click the **Change/Remove** button.

5. Click **Yes** to confirm the removal.

   The UninstallShield program runs and displays a list of the removed components on your computer.

   Which of the following items were removed by the uninstall program? (Select all that apply.)

   ❑　　　Program folders

   ❑　　　Registry entries

   ❑　　　User data

   ❑　　　Shared files

6. Click **OK**, then **Close**.

4.2.2 REMOVE A PROGRAM 1

Scenario

You have an evaluation copy of the WinZip program. You have finished the evaluation and need to remove the program from your system.

Your task in this lab is:

- Remove the WinZip program from your computer using the Add/Remove Programs applet.

Steps

Complete the following steps:

1. Click **Start/Settings/Control Panel**.

2. Double-click **Add/Remove Programs**. The following dialog is shown.

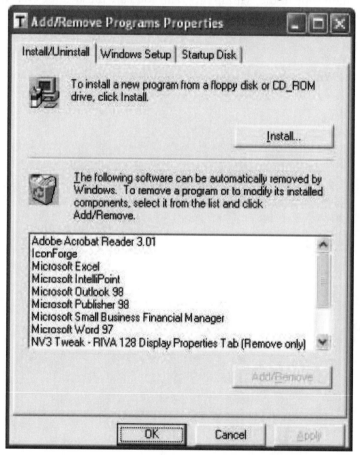

3. Scroll down the list of installed software and select the **WinZip** program. Click the **Add/ Remove** button.

4. Click **Yes**, then **Yes** again to uninstall the program.

5. Click **OK**.

4.2.3 REMOVE A PROGRAM 2

Scenario

You have completed the TestOut A+ Operating System course and have decided to remove the related files from your system.

Your task in this lab is:

- To remove the A+ Operating System course from your computer using the Add/Remove Program applet.

Steps

Complete the following steps:

1. Click **Start/Settings/Control Panel**.

2. Double-click **Add/Remove Programs**.

3. On the **Install/Uninstall** tab, scroll down the list of installed software and select the **TestOut A+ Operating System Course** entry. Click the **Add/Remove** button.

4. Accept the default uninstall action and click **Next**.

5. Click **Finish**.

5.0

Installing Hardware

5.1.2 INSTALL A DEVICE WITH THE ADD HARDWARE WIZARD

Scenario

You are installing a legacy network adapter on a Windows XP Professional computer. You have physically installed the network adapter, downloaded an appropriate driver from the manufacturer, and stored the driver in the D:\Network folder. The model of the network adapter is a 3Com EtherLink III ISA (3C509/3C509b).

Your task in this lab is to install the driver you downloaded for the legacy network adapter.

Steps

Complete the following steps:

1.   Click **Start**, then right-click **My Computer** and select **Properties** from the menu.

2.   Click the **Hardware** tab. The following dialog is shown.

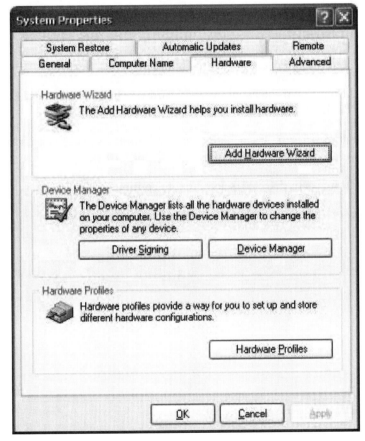

3.   Click the **Add Hardware Wizard** button.

     What is the recommended method of installing hardware?

_____

4. Click **Next** to begin the wizard. The wizard will scan for new Plug and Play hardware, but should not find any unless you recently added new Plug and Play hardware.

5. Select **No, I have not added the hardware yet** and click **Next**.

   What should you do before running the Add Hardware wizard?

   _____

6. Click **Back**.

7. Select **Yes, I have already connected the hardware**. Click **Next**.

8. Scroll to the bottom of the list of installed hardware devices and select **Add a new hardware device**. Click **Next**.

9. To let Windows perform legacy hardware search routines, select **Search for and install the hardware automatically (Recommended)**. Click **Next**.

10. If the hardware is not detected, select **Next** to continue.

11. Select **Network adapters** as the device type to install. Click **Next**.

12. Click the **Have Disk...** button. The following dialog is shown.

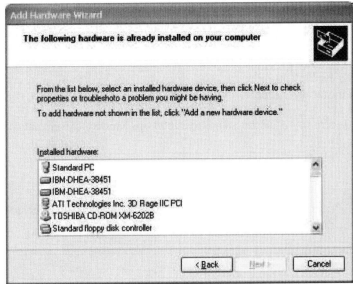

13. Click the **Browse** button.

14. Browse to the **D:\Network** folder and make sure the **Oemsetup.inf** file is selected. Click **Open**.

15. Click **OK**.

16. Click **Next**, then **Next** again to install the driver.

17. Click **Finish** to end the wizard.

18. To verify that the device has been installed, in the System Properties applet click the **Device Manager** button.

19. Expand the **Network adapters** node to view the newly-installed device.

Before using the Add Hardware wizard, what are two installation methods you should try first?

_____

_____

5.1.3 REMOVE A DEVICE

Scenario

You just installed a new Plug and Play modem on a Windows XP Professional computer. Previously, the computer used a legacy modem.

Your task in this lab is to uninstall the Standard 33600 bps Modem driver that was used by the legacy modem.

Steps

You must uninstall drivers for legacy devices manually (Plug and Play drivers are usually uninstalled automatically when you remove the hardware).

Complete the following steps:

1. Click **Start**, then right-click **My Computer** and select **Manage** to open the Computer Management console.

2. In **Device Manager**, expand the **Modems** node. Browse to the device you want to uninstall.

3. Right-click the device and select **Uninstall**.

4. Click **OK** to confirm.

5. To verify that the device was uninstalled, expand the **Modems** category.

5.1.4 INSTALL A PLUG AND PLAY DEVICE

Scenario

While troubleshooting a Windows XP Professional computer, you deleted the driver for a Plug and Play device. You now want Windows to redetect the device and install the driver. You want to do this without shutting down the computer.

Your task in this lab is to trigger Plug and Play detection without restarting the computer.

Steps

Complete the following steps:

1. Click **Start**, then right-click **My Computer** and select **Manage** to open the Computer Management console.

2. Click the **Device Manager** node.

   Notice that the **Modems** category doesn't currently exist.

3. Right-click any node in **Device Manager** and select **Scan for hardware changes**.

4. To verify that the device was detected, expand the **Modems** category and view the new device.

   What kind of modem did the scan detect?

   _____

5.2.2 UPDATE A DRIVER

Scenario

You are configuring a Windows XP Professional computer. You recently downloaded an updated driver from the display adapter manufacturer. The updated driver is stored in the D:\Video folder.

Your task in this lab is to update the display adapter to use the driver you downloaded.

Steps

Complete the following steps:

1. Click **Start**, then right-click **My Computer** and select **Manage** to open the Computer Management console.

2. Under **System Tools** select **Device Manager**.

3. Expand the **Display adapters** node. Right-click the device whose driver you want to update and choose **Properties**.

4. Click the **Driver** tab. The following dialog is shown.

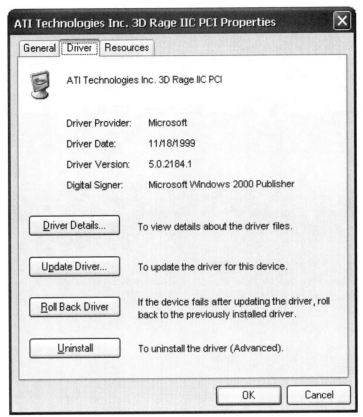

Note the current driver date and version number.

5. Click the **Update Driver...** button.

6. Because you have downloaded the device driver, select **Install from a list or specific location (Advanced)**. The Advanced option lets you customize where Windows looks for updated drivers, or you can choose the driver to install manually. Click **Next**.

7. To search in a specific folder, select the **Include this location in the search** option and click the **Browse** button.

8. Expand **My Computer** and browse and select the **D:\Video** folder. Click **OK**.

9. Click **Next** to continue.

10. Click **Finish** to close the wizard.

Note the new driver date and version number.

_____

5.3.2 ENABLE OR DISABLE A DEVICE

Scenario

While troubleshooting a Windows XP Professional computer, you disabled a driver for a device. You now want to enable the device and disable a different driver.

Your task in this lab is to:

- Enable the 3Com EtherLink XL 10/100 PCI NIC (3C905-TX) network adapter.

- Disable the 3Com Windows Modem T1 modem.

Steps

Complete the following steps:

1. Click **Start**, then right-click **My Computer** and select **Manage** to open the Computer Management console.

2. Click the **Device Manager** node.

3. Under the **Network Adapters** node, right-click the network adapter and select **Enable**.

4. Expand the **Modems** node. Right-click the modem and select **Disable**.

5. Click **Yes** to confirm the action.

   What type of icon indicates a disabled device?

   _____

5.4.2 CONFIGURE A LOCAL PRINTER (WIN98)

Scenario

You have just bought a Canon BJ-20 and have connected the printer to your computer. Now you are going to set up the printer to be used only by yourself.

Your tasks are:

- Add a printer.

- Set it as a local printer.

- Install the appropriate printer driver.

- Set the printer port to LPT1.

- Accept the default printer name.

- Make this the default printer.

- Do not print a test page.

Steps

Complete the following steps:

1. Click **Start/Settings/Printers**.

2. Double-click the **Add Printer** icon to start the Add Printer Wizard.

3. Click **Next** to begin.

4. Accept the default of **Local Printer** and click **Next**.

5. Select the manufacturer and printer model. When you are finished, the dialog should resemble the following:

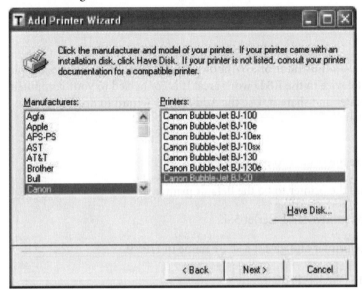

Click **Next**.

6. Select the port as required by the scenario and click **Next**.

7. Accept the default printer name, select **Yes** to make it the default printer, and click **Next**.

8. Select **No** when you are asked if you want to print a test page. Click **Finish**.

   How can you tell the difference between the default printer and a non-default printer?

5.4.4 CONFIGURE A LOCAL PRINTER (WINNT)

Scenario

You are a network administrator of a Windows NT 4.0 network. You have just placed a new HP LaserJet 5Si print device in the R&D work area. It is connected to your computer. You need to configure this printer and share it. Use the Add Printer wizard to do this.

Your tasks are:

- Configure the printer to use port LPT1.

- Configure the printer to be the default printer.

- Name the printer HP LaserJet 5Si.

- Share the printer and give it a share name of HP5Si.

- Do not print a test page.

You are already logged on as Administrator.

Steps

Complete the following steps:

1. Click **Start/Settings/Printers**.

2. Double-click the **Add Printer** icon.

3. Verify that **My Computer** is selected, then click **Next**.

4. In the **Available Ports** list, check **LPT1**. Click **Next**.

5. Select the manufacturer and printer model, then click **Next**.

6. Accept the default printer name. Click **Yes** to select the printer as the default printer. Click **Next**.

7. Click **Shared** and type **HP5Si** for the shared printer name. Click **Next**.

8. Click **No** so the Add Printer Wizard doesn't print a test page and click **Finish**.

5.4.6 INSTALL A PLUG AND PLAY PRINTER (WIN2000/XP)

Scenario

You are configuring the printing environment for a Windows XP Professional computer. You have attached a parallel print device to the computer's LPT1 port and turned the print device on. The print device is Plug and Play compatible.

Your task in this lab is to add a local printer for the print device. Accept the default settings. You do not need to print a test page.

Steps

In this scenario, you need to create a new local printer. Do this by autodetecting the printer and accepting the default settings.

Complete the following steps:

1. Click **Start**, then click **Printers and Faxes**.

2. Click the **Add a printer** task in the Printer Tasks list.

    How should you install a printer connected to a USB port?

    _____

3. Click **Next** to begin the Add Printer wizard.

4. The **Local printer attached to this computer** is selected by default. Also notice the **Automatically detect and install my Plug and Play printer** option is enabled. Click **Next**. Windows should detect the print device and install an appropriate driver.

5. Select **No** to skip printing a test page, then click **Next**.

6. Click **Finish**.

5.4.7 MANUALLY INSTALL A PRINTER (WIN2000/XP)

Scenario

You are configuring the printing environment for a Windows XP Professional computer. You have purchased the print device, but it has not yet arrived. The user will connect the print device to the local printer port after it arrives. Meanwhile, the user wants to send some print jobs to the printer's print queue. The user will pause the print queue and unpause it after connecting the print device.

Your task in this lab is to manually add a local printer using the following properties:

- Port = LPT1

- Manufacturer = HP

- Model= HP LaserJet 5Si

- Name = Dev-Prn2

- Shared = No

You do not need to print a test page.

Steps

In this scenario, you need to create the local printer manually.

Complete the following steps:

1. Click **Start**, then click **Printers and Faxes**.

2. In the Printer Tasks list, select the **Add a printer** task.

3. Click **Next** to begin the Add Printer wizard.

4.　Clear the **Automatically detect and install my Plug and Play printer** option, then click **Next**. The following dialog is shown:

5.　Select the printer port. Click **Next**.

6.　Select the printer manufacturer and the model from the corresponding lists. Click **Next**.

7.　Type the printer name and click **Next**.

8.　Accept the default sharing behavior and click **Next**.

9.　Select whether to print a test page (in the simulation, printing a test page has no effect). Click **Next**.

10. Click **Finish** to complete the Add Printer wizard.

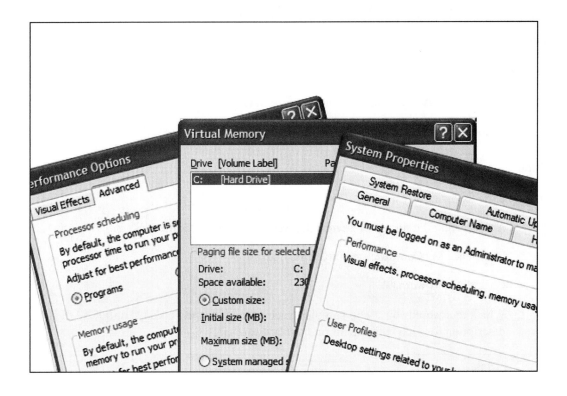

6.0

Managing and Optimizing Windows

6.2.8 USE THE SYSTEM APPLET

Scenario

Your client's network card has been disabled. Your task is:

- Enable the network card.

Steps

Complete the following steps:

1. After starting the simulator, review the scenario and click **Continue**.

2. Right-click **My Computer** and select **Properties**.

3. Click the **Hardware** tab.

   Which tool would you use to complete each of the following tasks? (Hint: Read the description for each component on the Hardware tab.)

Task	Tool
Configure and store multiple hardware configurations	
Install or repair hardware	
View installed devices and modify device properties	

4. Click the **Device Manager...** button.

5. Browse to view the installed hardware devices.

    What devices are installed for each of the following hardware categories?

Hardware Types	Devices Installed
DVD/CD-ROM drives	
Mice	
Network adapters	
Sound, video and game controllers	
Universal Serial Bus controllers	

6. Right-click the **3Com EtherLink XL 10/100 PCI NIC** network card and select **Enable**.

6.2.9 CHANGE THE COMPUTER NAME

Scenario

You have just received a Windows 2000 computer and want to use it as one of the testing computers.

Your task in this lab:

- Rename the computer to TestStation10.

Steps

Complete the following steps:

1. After starting the simulator, review the scenario and click **Continue**.

2. Right click **My Computer** and select **Properties**.

3. Click the **Network Identification** tab.

4. Click the **Properties** button. The following dialog is show.

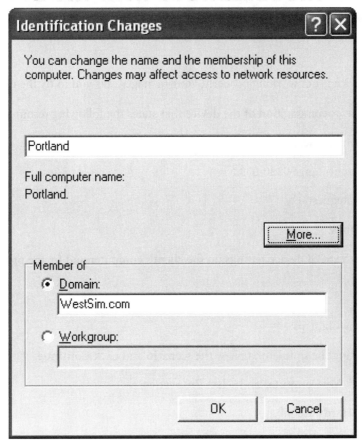

5. Type the new computer name and click **OK**.

6. Click **OK** again.

    Note: On a live system you would need to reboot before the change takes effect.

6.2.10 TROUBLESHOOT WITH THE SYSTEM APPLET

Scenario

A client's SCSI device is not working properly. Your manager asks you to fix the problem.

You have found the documentation of the device that states the following resource settings:

- Direct Memory Access 07
- Input/Output Range 0330-0333
- Interrupt Request 09

Your task in this lab is:

- Examine the SCSI device settings on the client's computer and fix the problem.

Steps

Complete the following steps:

1. After starting the simulator, review the scenario and click **Continue**.

2. Right-click **My Computer** and select **Properties**.

3. Click the **Hardware** tab.

4. Click the **Device Manager...** button.

   What icon is displayed in front of the SCSI Adapter to identify a problem with the device?

   _____

5. Right-click at the **SCSI Adapter--Adaptec AHA-154/AHA-164X SCSI Host adapter** and select **Properties**.

   What is the error code associated with the device?

   _____

6. Click the **Resources** tab.

7. Click the **Set Configuration Manually** button. The following information is shown.

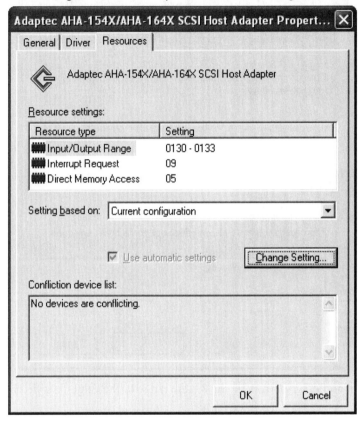

8. With **Input/Output Range** selected, click the **Change Setting...** button. The following dialog is shown.

9. Use the up and down arrows to change the range to the value specified by the scenario. Click **OK**.

10. Verify that the **Interrupt Request** resource is set to the value required by the scenario.

11. Select the **Direct Memory Access** resource and click the **Change Setting...** button.

12. Use the up and down arrows to change the range to the value specified by the scenario. Click **OK**.

13. Click **OK**, then **Yes** to make the changes.

How can you tell that the problem with the SCSI device should be solved?

_____

6.2.12 RESTART A SERVICE

Scenario

You are configuring a Windows XP Professional computer. You recently installed a DNS server on your network. After installing the DNS server, you configured the DNS server address on network clients manually. After setting the DNS server address on this Windows XP Professional computer, the computer still cannot resolve DNS hostnames. You want to fix the problem by restarting the DNS Client service.

Your task in this lab is to restart the DNS Client service.

Steps

Complete the following steps:

1. Click **Start**, then right-click **My Computer** and select **Manage** to open the Computer Management preconfigured MMC console.

2. Expand **Services and Applications** and click **Services**.

   Circle the services listed here that are currently started.

Fax	IISAdmin	Net Logon
Print Spooler	Telnet	WebClient

3. Right-click the service you want to restart and select **Restart** from the menu. This is the same as selecting **Stop**, then selecting **Start**.

   Note: You can also restart a service by editing the properties of a service and selecting **Stop** then **Start** on the General tab.

6.3.3 SET PRINT JOB PRIORITY

Scenario

Sandy from the Sales department has sent an invoice to the network printer. She needs to have the invoice immediately. However, there are a lot of print jobs in the queue. She comes to you for help.

Your task is:

- Change Sandy's print job's priority to the highest possible priority.

Steps

Complete the following steps:

1. After starting the simulator, review the scenario and click **Continue**.

2. Click **Start/Settings/Printers**.

3. Double-click the **HP LaserJet 5Si** printer to open the print queue.

   How many documents are in the print queue?

   _____

   Which user printed the **Test Results** document?

   _____

   Which document is the largest?

   _____

4. Right-click document that Sandy printed and select **Properties** from the menu. The
    following dialog is shown:

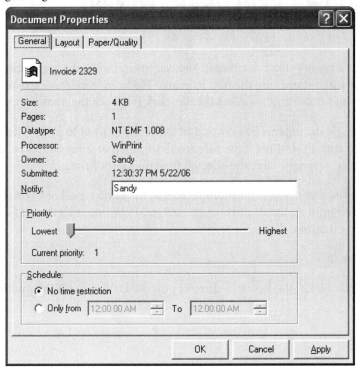

5. Drag the Priority bar from **Lowest** to **Highest**.

    What is the value of the **Current priority** when you have selected the highest priority?

    _____

6. Click **OK** to close the Properties box.

6.3.4 PRINT MULTIPLE DOCUMENTS FROM WINDOWS EXPLORER (WIN98)

Scenario

There are different ways to print a document. You can print it from the application and from Windows explorer without opening the file. To print a file from Windows explorer, select the file, right-click the file and click Print; or select the file, click File from the Menu bar, then click Print.

You can print multiple documents by selecting all the files you want to print (click the first file and press shift and click the last file if the files are all together, or press ctrl and click the desired files if they are scattered), right-click the selected files, then click Print.

Note: you can only do this if you print multiple files of the same type. For example, you can use this print method to print all the documents created in MS Word, or all the txt files or the graphic files with the same extension.

Your task in this lab is:

- Print all text files in the Research directory on the D: drive with the multiple selection method.

Steps

Complete the following steps:

1. Right-click **Start** and click **Explore**.

2. Browse and select the **D:\Research** directory.

3. Press the Ctrl key and click all of the **.txt** files in this directory.

4. Right-click the selected files and choose **Print**.

6.3.5 PRINT SELECTED DOCUMENTS FROM WINDOWS EXPLORER (WIN98)

Scenario

There are different ways to print a document. You can print it from the application and from Windows explorer without opening the file. To print a file from Windows explorer, select the file, right-click the file and click Print; or select the file, click File from the Menu bar, then click Print.

You can print multiple documents by selecting all the files you want to print (click the first file and press shift and click the last file if the files are all together, or press ctrl and click the selected files if they are scattered.), and right-click the selected files, then click Print.

Note: you can only do this if you print multiple files of the same type. For example, you can use this print method to print all the documents created in MS Word, or all the txt files or the graphic files with the same extension.

Your task in this lab is:

- Use multiple selection method to print Design.rtf and Production.rtf in the Process Improvements directory on the D: drive.

Steps

Complete the following steps:

1. Right-click **Start** and click **Explore**.

2. Browse and select the **D:\Process Improvements** directory.

3. Press the Ctrl key and click the **Design.rtf** and **Production.rtf** files.

4. Right-click the selected files and choose **Print**.

6.3.6 CHANGE THE DEFAULT PRINTER

Scenario

You are configuring the printing environment for a Windows XP Professional computer. By default, you want the computer to print to a local printer attached to the computer.

Your task in this lab is to configure the Dev-Prn2 printer to be the computer's default printer.

Steps

Complete the following steps:

1. Click **Start**, then click **Printers and Faxes**.

    What is the current default printer?

    _____

2. Right-click the **Dev-Prn2** and select **Set as Default Printer**.

6.3.7 CANCEL A PRINT JOB

Scenario

You manage a Windows XP Professional computer that has a shared printer. User SBlack has submitted a large print job to the shared printer. Due to other users' complaints, you want to delete the print job. You will ask SBlack to resend the print job after hours.

Your task in this lab is to delete user SBlack's print job named Research Results on this computer's shared printer.

Steps

In this scenario, you need to cancel the Research Results print job that is being printed by the Dev-Prn2 printer.

Complete the following steps:

1. Click **Start**, then click **Printers and Faxes**.

2. Right-click the printer and select **Open**. The following dialog is shown:

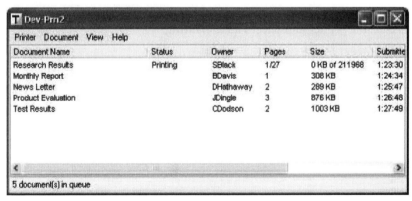

3. Right-click the **Research Results** document and select **Cancel**.

   Note: You can also select the print job you want to cancel and press the **Delete** key.

6.3.8 PAUSE PRINT JOBS

Scenario

The printer service technician needs to perform maintenance on the HP LaserJet 5Si printer. However, there are a lot of print jobs in the queue. He comes to you for help.

Your task is:

- Pause the HP LaserJet 5Si printer.

Steps

Complete the following steps:

1. After starting the simulator, review the scenario and click **Continue**.

2. Click **Start/Settings/Printers**.

   What is the current status of the HP LaserJet 5Si printer?

   _____

3. Right-click the printer and select **Pause Printing**.

6.4.2 CONFIGURE POWER OPTIONS FOR A PRESENTATION

Scenario

You are setting up a Windows 2000 portable computer for a presentation at a conference. You want the computer to stay on all the time during the presentation no matter how long the computer stands idle.

Your tasks in the lab are:

*   Configure the computer with Presentation scheme.

Steps

Complete the following steps:

1. After starting the simulator, review the scenario and click **Continue**.

2. Click **Start**, then select **Settings/Control Panel**.

3.   Double-click **Power Options**. The following dialog is shown:

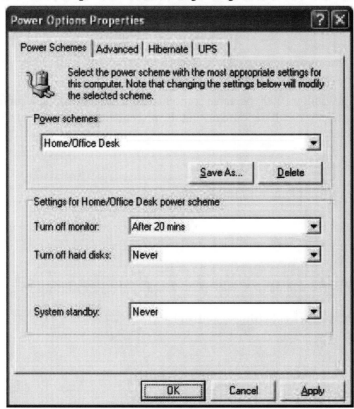

4.   In the **Power schemes** box, select **Presentation**.

What is the difference between the Presentation scheme and the Home/Office Desk scheme?

_____

5.   Click **OK**.

6.4.3 CONFIGURE POWER OPTIONS FOR A LAPTOP

Scenario

You are going on a business trip and need to take your laptop computer. To save battery power, you want to configure the monitor and hard drive to shut off after a certain period of time.

Your tasks in the lab are:

- Configure the computer with Portable/Laptop scheme.

Steps

Complete the following steps:

1. After starting the simulator, review the scenario and click **Continue**.

2. Click **Start**, then select **Settings/Control Panel**.

3. Double-click **Power Options**.

4. In the Power schemes box, select the various preconfigured power schemes to complete the following table.

Power Scheme	Turn off monitor	Turn off hard disks	System standby
Home/Office Desk			
Portable/Laptop			
Presentation			
Max Battery			

5. In the **Power schemes** box, select **Portable/Laptop**, then click **OK**.

6.4.4 CREATE A CUSTOM POWER CONFIGURATION

Scenario

You are going on a business trip and need to take your laptop computer. To save battery power, you want to configure the monitor and hard drive to shut off after a certain period of time. You decide to create your own custom power configuration.

Your tasks in the lab are:

- Configure the settings so that the monitor will be turned off after it is idle for 5 minutes.

- Configure the settings so that the hard disk will be turned off after it is idle for 5 minutes.

- Configure the settings so that the system will be in Standby Mode after the computer is idle for 20 minutes.

- Save the configuration with the name: My Settings.

Steps

Complete the following steps:

1. After starting the simulator, review the scenario and click **Continue**.

2. Click **Start,** then select **Settings/Control Panel**.

3. Double-click **Power Options**.

4. Configure the following settings:

   ◦ For **Turn off monitor**, select **After 5 mins**.

   ◦ For **Turn off hard disks**, select **After 5 mins**.

   ◦ For System standby, select **After 20 mins**.

5. Click the **Save As…** button.

6. Type the name for the custom power scheme, then click **OK**.

7. Click **OK**.

6.5.1 CONFIGURE VIRTUAL MEMORY

Scenario

For virtual-memory support, Windows 2000 creates one paging file called Pagefile.sys on the disk or volume on which the operating system is installed.

Because the size and location of paging files can affect your system's performance, you might want to modify them.

You decide to set a paging file on the D: drive and leave a small paging file on the C: drive to improve the performance of your system.

Your tasks in the lab are:

1. Change minimum and maximum size of the paging file on the C: drive to the minimum size that still allows debugging information to be written on the C: drive (127 MB).

2. Set a paging file on the D: drive with the initial size for the swap file to 192 MB and the maximum size to 384 MB.

Steps

Complete the following steps:

1.   After starting the simulator, review the scenario and click **Continue**.

2. Right click **My Computer** and click **Properties**.

3. Click the **Advanced** tab.

4. Click the **Performance Options...** button.

    What is the current paging size for all drives on this system?

    _____

5. To change virtual memory settings, click the **Change...** button. The following dialog is shown:

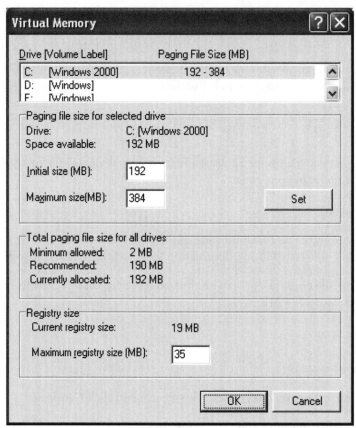

6. To change the size of the file on the C: drive, with the drive selected, set the **Initial size (MB)** and **Maximum size (MB)** values to **127**. Click the **Set** button.

7. To add a paging file to the D: drive, select the drive and configure the initial and maximum sizes, then click **Set**.

8. Click **OK**, then **OK** again.

6.5.2 TROUBLESHOOT MEMORY PROBLEMS

Scenario

You have experienced out of memory errors recently when trying to run an application. The error does not seem to be isolated to specific programs. You have checked the amount of physical memory available to Windows. There appears to be sufficient physical memory. You check the percentage of free memory, and notice that the percentage of available memory is high. Still you cannot run the program. You want to check the virtual memory settings.

Your tasks in the lab are:

- Check the C: drive to see if there is enough space for the page file.

- If there is enough space on the C: drive, increase the initial size of the pagefile to 384 MB. If there is not enough space, reduce the minimum and maximum sizes of the page file on the C: drive to minimum allowed for debugging information to be written to the C: drive (127 MB).

- Specify an alternative drive if necessary.

- Make sure that the sum total of the initial page file sizes on all drives to 384 MB.

Steps

Complete the following steps:

1. After starting the simulator, review the scenario and click **Continue**.

2. Right click **My Computer** and click **Properties**.

3. Click the **Advanced** tab.

4. Click the **Performance Options...** button.

5. To view and change the virtual memory settings, click the **Change...** button.

    Examine the current settings and the scenario requirements. Complete the following table with the current and recommended changes.

Drive	Disk space available	Current Setting		New Setting	
		Initial size	Maximum size	Initial size	Maximum size
C:					
D:					
E:					

    Note: In this lab, you can choose which additional drive to use if you need extra space for the paging file.

6. To change the paging file settings, select a drive, set the initial and maximum sizes, then click the **Set** button.

7. Repeat step 6 as necessary to configure additional paging files on other drives.

8. Click **OK** to save the changes.

9. Click **OK**.

6.7.2 VIEW REGISTRY FILES

Scenario

In this lab, you need to perform the following tasks:

- Open Regedit and examine the Registry structure

- Open Regedt32 and view the registry in Read Only Mode

Click the **Done** button after you finish these tasks.

Steps

Complete the following steps:

1. After starting the simulator, review the scenario and click **Continue**.

2. Click **Start/Run...**.

3. In the Run box, type **regedit** and click **OK**.

4. Close the registry editor.

5. To open Regedt32 in Read Only mode, click **Start/Run...**.

6. Type **regedt32** and click **OK**.

    How does the information you see in **Regedt32** differ from what was shown in **Regedit**?

    _____

7. To view the registry in Read Only mode, from the **Options** menu select **Read Only Mode**.

7.0

Networking

7.1.3 CREATE A DIRECT CONNECTION (GUEST)

Scenario

You want to transfer some files between a Windows XP Professional laptop computer and a Windows XP Professional desktop computer. Unfortunately, the laptop computer does not have a working network card. You decide to connect the two computers using a null modem cable connected directly between the two computers' serial (COM) ports.

Your task in this lab is to create a direct connection on the Windows XP Professional laptop computer that accesses the desktop computer as a guest. Configure the connection to use the following properties:

- Host Computer Name/Connection Name = LA-CORP-WRK3
- Device = COM1

Steps

In this lab, create a new network connection. During the wizard, select the advanced connection option, and configure the computer to connect as a guest.

Complete the following steps:

1. Click **Start**, then right-click **My Network Places** and select **Properties**.

2. In the **Network Connections** folder, select the **Create a new connection** network task.

3. Click **Next** to start the New Connection wizard.

   Which connection type would you select to create a dial-up connection?

   _____

4. Select **Set up an advanced connection**. Click **Next**.

5. Select **Connect directly to another computer** and click **Next**.

6. Select **Guest** as the role for the computer, then click **Next**.

7. Type the name of the computer to which you are connecting (this determines the name of the network connection). Click **Next**.

8. Select a port from the **Select a device:** list. Click **Next**.

9. Click **Finish** to create the connection.

7.1.4 CREATE A DIRECT CONNECTION (HOST)

Scenario

You want to transfer some files between a Windows XP Professional laptop computer and a Windows XP Professional desktop computer. Unfortunately, the laptop computer does not have a working network card. You decide to connect the two computers using a null modem cable connected directly between the two computers' serial (COM) ports.

Your task in this lab is to configure the Windows XP Professional desktop computer to host an incoming connection over the computer's COM1 serial port. Configure an incoming connection using the following properties:

- Device(s) = COM1

- Authorized user account(s) = Administrator

Steps

You can create only a single incoming connection on a Windows XP Professional computer. This connection is used to identify the properties for *all* incoming connections through any connection medium (direct connections using COM, LPT, or IrDA ports; dial-up connections; or VPN connections). Use the New Connection wizard in Network Connections to create the incoming connection. If you are configuring a direct connection, the simplest method to use is to make the following choices during the wizard:

1. Select an advanced connection.

2. Select a direct connection as the connection type.

3. Configure the computer as the host computer for the connection.

Complete the following steps:

1. Click **Start**, then right-click **My Network Places** and select **Properties**.

2. Select the **Create a new connection** network task.

3. Click **Next** to start the New Connection wizard.

4. Select **Set up an advanced connection**, then click **Next**.

5. Select **Connect directly to another computer** and click **Next**.

6. Accept **Host** as the role for the computer, then click **Next**.

7. Accept **Communications Port (Com1)** as the port, then click **Next**. The following dialog is shown:

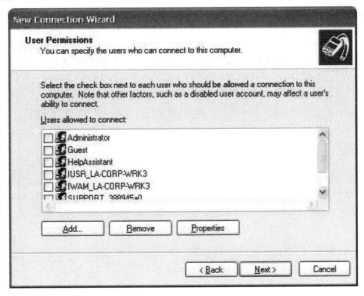

8. Select the check box for the local user account that is permitted to establish an incoming connection. To establish a connection to the computer, users will have to supply the user name and password of a user account that you select. Click **Next** to continue.

9. Click **Finish** to create the connection.

7.1.5 UNINSTALL A NETWORK COMPONENT

Scenario

You are configuring network connections for a Windows XP Professional computer. Previously, the company used Novell NetWare servers. All NetWare servers have now been migrated to Windows 2000 servers, so the Client Service for NetWare installed on this computer is no longer needed.

Your task in this lab is to uninstall the Client Service for NetWare client software.

Steps

Complete the following steps:

1. Click **Start**. Right-click **My Network Places** and select **Properties**.

2. In the **Network Connections** folder, right-click a connection and select **Properties**.

    Note: In most cases, you can uninstall components from the properties of any connection. However, you cannot uninstall some components from the properties of a dial-up connection.

    What components are currently installed?

    _____

    _____

    _____

3. Select the **Client Service for Netware** component. Click **Uninstall**.

4. Click **Yes** to confirm the action to remove the component.

5. On an actual Windows system, you would now be prompted to reboot the system. Click **OK**.

6. To confirm the action, right-click the network connection and select **Properties**.

    Which components were removed?

    _____

    _____

    _____

7.2.2 CONFIGURE TCP/IP SETTINGS

Scenario

You are connecting a Windows XP Professional computer to your network. Currently, your network uses manual IP addressing.

Your task in this lab is to configure the TCP/IP properties for the Local Area Connection network connection to use the following static values:

- IP Address = 192.168.1.6

- Subnet Mask = 255.255.255.0

- Default Gateway = 192.168.1.254

Steps

Complete the following steps:

1. Click **Start**, then right-click **My Network Places** and select **Properties**.

2. In the **Network Connections** folder, right-click the network connection and select **Properties** from the menu.

3. Select **Internet Protocol (TCP/IP)** from the list of items used by the connection, then click the **Properties** button. The following graphic is shown.

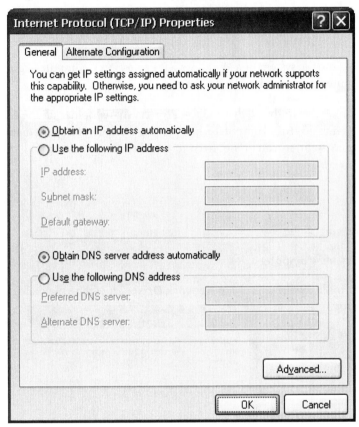

4. Select the **Use the following IP address** option and enter the IP address, subnet mask, and default gateway values. Click **OK**.

5. Click **OK** again to close the properties of the network connection.

7.3.1 MAP A DRIVE TO A SHARED FOLDER

Scenario

You are configuring the file system of a Windows XP Professional computer. You want to map a drive on this computer to a shared folder on the network.

Your task in this lab is to map the N: drive to the Projects shared folder on the NY-DEV-WRK3 computer. (The NY-DEV-WRK3 computer is part of the Westsim.Private domain.) Make sure the drive mapping is persistent, so you do not need to establish the drive mapping manually every time you log on.

Steps

Complete the following steps:

1.   Click **Start/My Computer**.

2.   From the **Tools** menu, select **Map Network Drive**. The following dialog is shown.

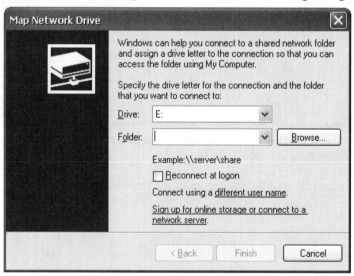

3.   Select the drive letter from the **Drive** list. To select the network shared folder, click the **Browse...** button.

4. Expand the **westsim.private** domain and the **NY-DEV-WRK3** computer.

5. Select the **Projects** folder and click **OK**.

6. Select **Reconnect at logon** to restore the drive mapping each time you log on. Click **Finish**.

   How does the mapped drive icon differ from a physical drive icon?

   _____

7.3.2 CONFIGURE A CLIENT FOR DHCP

Scenario

You are configuring network connections for a Windows XP Professional computer. Previously, your network did not have a DHCP server, but you have just installed and configured one.

Your task in this lab is to configure the TCP/IP protocol for the Local Area Connection network connection to get IP addressing and DNS server information from the DHCP server.

Steps

Complete the following steps:

1. Click **Start**, then right-click **My Network Places** and select **Properties**.

2. In the **Network Connections** folder, right-click the network connection and select **Properties**.

3. Select **Internet Protocol (TCP/IP)** from the list of items used by the connection. Click the **Properties** button.

4. Make the following changes:

   ○ Select the **Obtain an IP address automatically** option. This option will use a DHCP server if one exists. Otherwise, it will use Automatic Private IP Addressing (APIPA) to assign an address between 169.254.0.0 and 169.254.255.255.

   ○ Select the **Obtain DNS server address automatically** option to obtain DNS server addresses from a DHCP server

   Click **OK** to save the changes.

5. Click **OK** again to close the properties of the network connection.

7.4.4 CREATE A LOCAL USER ACCOUNT

Scenario

You are configuring local users and groups for a Windows XP Professional computer that is a member of a workgroup. You want to create a user account for a new employee. The new employee will not start for a few days, so you want to keep the account disabled for now.

Your task in this lab is to create a new local user account with the following properties:

- User Name = sbagley
- Full Name = Sue Bagley
- Description = Lead Designer
- Password = sbagley
- User must change password at next logon = True
- Account is disabled = True

Steps

Many of the user account properties required in this scenario (such as setting the full name, description, and disabling the account) can only be set by using the Local Users and Groups snap-in.

Complete the following steps:

1. Click **Start**, then right-click **My Computer** and select **Manage** to open the Computer Management preconfigured MMC console.

2. Expand **System Tools**, then expand **Local Users and Groups**.

3. Right-click the **Users** folder and select **New User...** from the menu. The New User dialog box is shown.

4. Configure the user account properties to meet the scenario requirements.

How can you enable the **User cannot change password** option to allow you to select it?

_____

Which option becomes disabled when you select the **Password never expires** option?

_____

5. Click **Create**. The New User dialog stays open so you can create additional user accounts.

6. Click **Close**.

7.4.5 CREATE A PASSWORD AND PASSWORD HINT

Scenario

You administer a Windows XP Professional computer that is a member of a workgroup. Sue Bagley, the user of this computer, does not have a password for her local user account. You want all user accounts to use passwords.

Your task in this lab is to create a password and password hint for Sue Bagley's user account. Set the password to *3257* and configure *Your employee ID (please change)* as a password hint.

Steps

When a computer is a member of a workgroup rather than a domain, you can set the account password using either the User Accounts applet in the Control Panel, or with Local Users and Groups in Computer Management. However, you can only configure a password hint for a user account using the User Accounts applet.

Complete the following steps:

1. Click **Start/Control Panel**.

2. Click **User Accounts**.

3. Click a user account.

4.   Select **Create a password**. The following screen is shown.

Create a password for sbagley's account

You are creating a password for sbagley. **If you do this, sbagley will lose all EFS-encrypted files, personal certificates, and stored passwords for Web sites or network resources.**

To avoid losing data in the future, ask sbagley to make a password reset floppy disk.

Type a new password:

Type the new password again to confirm:

If the password contains capital letters, they must be typed the same way every time.

Type a word or phrase to use as a   password hint:

The password hint will be visible to everyone who uses this computer.

[Create Password]   [Cancel]

5.   Type the password (twice) and a password hint. Click **Create Password**.

7.4.6 CONFIGURE PASSWORD RESTRICTIONS

Scenario

You are the administrator for a small non-domain network. You want to improve the password security of your own Windows XP Professional workstation. Use the Local Security Policy tool and configure the following password restrictions:

- Passwords must be 8 characters

- Passwords must be changed every 30 days

- Passwords must contain non-alphabetical characters

Note: Policy changes will not be enforced within the lab.

Steps

Complete the following table with the necessary settings for this scenario.

Password Policy	Setting
Minimum password length	
Maximum password age	
Password must meet complexity requirements	

Complete the following steps:

1. Click **Start/Administrative Tools/Local Security Policy**.

2. In the Local Security Policy editor, browse to **Account Policies/Password Policy**.

3. In the right window, right-click the **Maximum password age** policy and select **Properties**. The following dialog is shown:

4. Configure the policy settings and click **OK**.

5. Repeat steps 3 and 4 to configure additional policies required by the scenario.

   What is the difference between the minimum password age and the maximum password age?

   _____

   Which setting would you configure to prevent users from re-using previous passwords?

   _____

7.4.7 CONFIGURE ACCOUNT LOCKOUT RESTRICTIONS

Scenario

You work at an architectural firm that has just secured a large contract. Part of the contract calls for increased security measures for all computers that store third-party data. Your computer is a non-domain member running Windows XP Professional.

Use the Local Security Policy editor to tighten the account lockout settings on your computer to help prevent hackers from gaining access to the system. Secure the system by locking user accounts after three incorrect logon attempts. Lock the system for 30 minutes, and reset the lockout counter after 45 minutes.

Steps

Complete the following table with the necessary settings for this scenario.

Account Lockout Policy	Setting
Account lockout duration	
Account lockout threshold	
Reset account lockout counter after	

Complete the following steps:

1. Click **Start/Administrative Tools/Local Security Policy**.

2. In the Local Security Policy editor, browse to **Account Policies/Account Lockout Policy**.

3. In the right window, right-click the policy you want to edit and select **Properties**.

4. Configure the policy settings and click **OK**.

5. Repeat steps 3 and 4 to configure additional policies.

   How long will an account be locked if the **Account lockout duration** is set to 0? (**Hint:** Configure the policy and read the setting description.)

   _____

7.4.8 CREATE A LIMITED USER ACCOUNT

Scenario

You are configuring local users and groups for a Windows XP Professional computer that is a member of a workgroup. You want to create a local user account for a new employee.

Your task in this lab is to create a new local user account with the following properties:

- User Name and Full Name = Sue Bagley
- Account Type = Limited

Steps

When a computer is a member of a workgroup, you can create users using the Local Users and Groups snap-in or the User Accounts applet in the Control Panel. In this scenario, the User Accounts applet is sufficient.

Complete the following steps:

1. Click **Start/Control Panel**.

2. Click **User Accounts**.

3. Select the **Create a new account** task.

4. Type a name for the new account. Then click **Next**. (The user name and full name will be set to the name you type.) The following dialog is shown:

5. Select the account type for the new user account.

   Which account type would you choose to create a user capable of doing the following tasks?

Task	Account Type
Access files created by the user	
Change the user password and picture	
Create and modify user accounts	
Install programs	
View files in the Shared Documents folder	

6. Click **Create Account**.

7.4.11 MODIFY GROUP MEMBERSHIP

Scenario

You administer a Windows XP Professional computer that is a member of a workgroup. Sue Bagley, the user of this computer, is currently a member of the Users local group. You want to delegate to Sue certain administrative tasks such as installing most applications and managing local users and groups.

Your task in this lab is to remove Sue Bagley's local user account from the Users local group and add it to the Power Users local group.

Steps

When a computer is a member of a workgroup, you can make a user account a computer administrator (member of the Administrators local group) or a limited user (member of the Users local group) using the User Accounts applet in the Control Panel. However, to perform other group membership tasks, you need to use the Local Users and Groups snap-in. When configuring group membership, you can do so by assigning groups to a user account or by assigning user accounts to a group. Both methods accomplish the same result.

Complete the following steps:

1. Click **Start**, then right-click **My Computer** and select **Manage** to open the Computer Management preconfigured MMC console.

2. Expand **System Tools**, then expand **Local Users and Groups**.

3. Select the **Users** folder.

4. Right-click the applicable user account and select **Properties**.

5. Click the **Member Of** tab. The following dialog is shown:

6. To add the user to a group, click **Add....**

   Note: On a real system you would be able to type the name of the group. This feature is not enabled in the simulation.

7. Click the **Advanced...** button.

8.   Click **Find Now** to display a list of local groups.

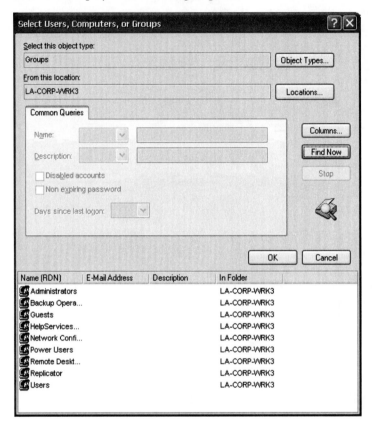

9.   Select the desired group and click **OK**. Click **OK** again to add the user to the group.

10. To remove a group, select the group and click **Remove**.

11. Click **OK**.

7.4.12 ADD A USER TO A LOCAL GROUP

Scenario

You administer a Windows XP Professional computer that is a member of a domain named Westsim.Private. You want to give Will Adams, a user in the Sales department, full control to this computer.

Your task in this lab is to add the Will Adams domain user account to this computer's Administrators local group.

Steps

When a computer is a member of a domain, you can add domain users to local groups by using the User Accounts applet in the Control Panel, or by using the Local Users and Groups snap-in.

Complete the following steps:

1. Click **Start**, then right-click **My Computer** and select **Manage** to open the Computer Management preconfigured MMC console.

2. Expand **System Tools**, then expand **Local Users and Groups**.

3. Select the **Groups** folder.

4. Right-click the applicable group and select **Properties** or **Add to group....**

5. On the General tab, click **Add....**

   Note: On a real system you would be able to type the name of the group. This feature is not enabled in the simulation.

6. Click the **Advanced...** button.

7. Click **Find Now**.

8. Select the desired user and click **OK**. Click **OK** again to add the user to the group.

9. Click **OK**.

7.4.13 CREATE A LOCAL GROUP AND ADD MEMBERS

Scenario

You administer a Windows XP Professional computer that is a member of an Active Directory domain named **Westsim.Private.** You want to grant members of the **Research, Sales,** and **Accounting** domain global groups permissions to several resources on this computer. To facilitate administration of permissions, you decide to apply all permissions via a local group on this computer.

Your task in this lab is create a new local group named **Domain Resource Access.** Add the **Research, Sales,** and **Accounting** domain global groups as members of the new local group.

Steps

Complete the following steps:

1. Click **Start**, then right-click **My Computer** and select **Manage** to open the Computer Management preconfigured MMC console.

2. Expand **System Tools**, then expand **Local Users and Groups**.

3. Right-click the **Groups** folder and select **New Group...** from the menu. The following dialog is shown:

4. Type the name and description for the new group.

5. To add group members, click **Add....**

   Note: On a real system you would be able to type the name of the group. This feature is not enabled in the simulation.

6. Click the **Advanced...** button.

7. Click **Find Now.**

8. Select the user or group that you want to add to the group. **Tip:** Hold down the Ctrl key to select multiple users or groups. Click **OK.**

9. Click **Create**. The New Group dialog remains open so you can create additional groups.

10. Click **Close.**

7.4.16 CHANGE USER RIGHTS

Scenario

You work for a hardware manufacturing firm that designs new PCI cards for the latest wireless technologies. One of the testers is responsible for installing and testing the hardware. The user account that she uses is a member of the Power Users group. Because of the nature of her work, her user account requires additional user rights on the local system.

Use the Local Security Policy editor to enable the Power Users local group to load and unload device drivers and to debug programs.

Steps

To enable Power Users to load and unload device drivers and debug programs, browse to **Local Policies/User Rights Assignment**. Add the Power Users group to the following policies:

- Debug programs

- Load and unload device drivers

Complete the following steps:

1. Click **Start/Administrative Tools/Local Security Policy**.

2. Browse to **Local Policies/User Rights Assignments**.

3. In the right window, double-click the **Debug Programs** policy. The following dialog is shown.

4. Click **Add User or Group…**.

5. Click the **Object Types…** button. The following dialog is shown:

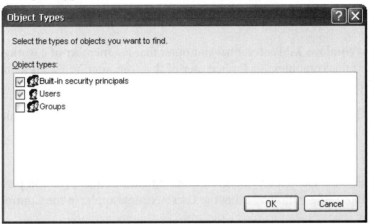

6. Check the box for **Groups** to include groups in the display. Click **OK**.

7. Click **Advanced…**, then **Find Now**.

8. Select **Power Users** and click **OK**.

9. Click **OK** to add the group, then **OK** again to close the policy setting and accept the changes.

10. Repeat steps 3 through 9 to define any additional policies.

7.4.17 CHANGE THE ACCOUNT TYPE

Scenario

You administer a Windows XP Professional computer that is a member of a workgroup. Sue Bagley, the user of this computer, is a limited user of this computer. You want to make her a computer administrator.

Your task in this lab is to change Sue Bagley's account type to be a computer administrator.

Steps

When a computer is a member of a workgroup rather than a domain, you can perform limited group membership configuration by using the User Accounts applet in the Control Panel. You have two options:

> 1. **Computer Administrator** makes the user a member of the Administrators local group.
>
> 2. **Limited** makes the user a member of the Users local group.

You could perform the same task by using the Local Users and Groups snap-in and modifying the group membership.

Complete the following steps:

1. Click **Start/Control Panel**.

2. Click **User Accounts**.

3. Select the **Sue Bagley** user account.

4. Select **Change the account type**. The following dialog is shown:

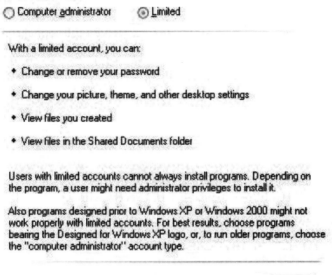

5. Select the **Computer Administrator** account type for the Sue Bagley user account.

6. Click **Change Account Type**.

7.4.18 ENABLE FAST USER SWITCHING

Scenario

You are configuring the logon environment for a Windows XP Professional computer that is a member of a workgroup. You want to let users put their work on hold and let other users log on.

Your task in this lab is to enable fast user switching for this computer.

Steps

When a computer is a member of a workgroup, you can let multiple users share a computer without requiring that each user log off. Instead, users can keep their programs open and switch to another user environment. This is called *Fast User Switching*. In this scenario, use the User Accounts applet in the Control Panel to enable Fast User Switching.

Complete the following steps:

1. Click **Start/Control Panel**.

2. Click **User Accounts**.

3. Select the **Change the way users log on or off** task. The following dialog is shown:

Select logon and logoff options

☑ **Use the Welcome screen**

By using the Welcome screen, you can simply click your account name to log on. For added security, you can turn off this feature and use the classic logon prompt which requires users to type a user account name.

☐ **Use Fast User Switching**

With Fast User Switching, you can quickly switch to another user account without having to close any programs. Then, when the other user is finished, you can switch back to your own account.

[Apply Options] [Cancel]

4. To enable fast user switching, do both of the following:

    ◦   If the **Use the Welcome screen** option is not enabled, enable it.

    ◦   Enable the **Fast User Switching** option.

    How can you configure the computer to use the classic logon prompt?

    _____

    Can you use the classic logon prompt and Fast User Switching at the same time?

    _____

5. Click **Apply Options**.

7.5.2 CONFIGURE SHARE PERMISSIONS

Scenario

You are configuring the file system of a Windows XP Professional computer. The D:\Projects folder is located on a FAT32 partition and has been shared using the share name Projects. You want to make sure that only users of the Research domain local group can read, write, and delete this shared folder's contents.

Your task in this lab is to configure share permissions for the Projects shared folder so that only members of the Research domain global group can view, change, and delete its contents.

Steps

Complete the following steps:

1. Click **Start/My Computer.**

2. Browse to the folder. Right-click it and select **Sharing and Security…**. The following dialog is shown:

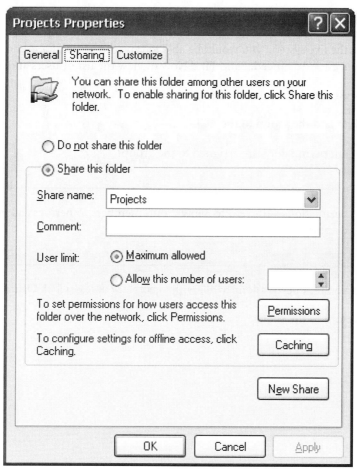

3. Click the **Permissions** button.

    What permissions are currently assigned to Everyone?

    _____

4. To prevent Everyone from accessing the share, select **Everyone** and click the **Remove** button.

5. Click **Add...** to add a group to the list.

6. **Note:** On the live system, you would be able to type the name of a user or a group. In the simulation, click **Advanced...** and **Find Now** to view the list of users and groups.

7. Select the **Research** group and click **OK**.

8. Click **OK** to add the group to the ACL.

    What default permissions are assigned to the group?

    _____

    Are these permissions sufficient to allow group members to perform all necessary tasks? Why or why not?

    _____

9. Check or uncheck permissions to allow the necessary access. Click **OK**.

10. Click **OK** to save the changes.

7.5.6 SHARE A FOLDER

Scenario

You are configuring the file system of a Windows XP Professional computer. The D:\Projects folder needs to be accessed by other users on the network. You have already configured appropriate NTFS permissions for the folder. Now you want to share the folder.

Your task in this lab is to share the D:\Projects folder using the share name *Projects*. Keep the default share permissions and other settings.

Steps

Complete the following steps:

1. Click **Start/My Computer**.

2. Navigate to the folder you want to share.

3. Right-click the folder and select **Sharing and Security....**

4. Select **Share this folder**.

5. Verify that **Projects** is the share name.

6. To view the share permissions, click **Permissions**.

    By default, what permissions does Everyone have to the Projects share?

    _____

7. Click **OK**.

8. Click **OK** again to begin sharing.

7.5.7 ACCESS A SHARED FOLDER

Scenario

You are using a Windows XP Professional computer. You want to delete a folder from another computer on the network.

Your task in this lab is to delete the Project1 folder and its contents from the Projects shared folder on the NY-DEV-WRK3 computer.

Steps

Complete the following steps:

1. Click **Start/Run…**.

2. Type the UNC path to the shared folder. Use the syntax: *computername**sharename*. Click **OK**.

3. Right-click the **Project1** folder and select **Delete**.

4. Click **Yes** to confirm.

7.5.9 SHARE A LOCAL PRINTER (WIN2000/XP)

Scenario

You are configuring the printing environment for a Windows XP Professional computer. You want to let other users on the network print to a local printer on the computer.

Your task in this lab is to share the Local LPT1 printer on this computer. Use a share name of Dev-Prn2 and make sure the printer is published to Active Directory.

Steps

Complete the following steps:

1. Click **Start/Printers and Faxes**.

2. Right-click the printer you want to share and select **Sharing and Security...** from the menu. The following dialog is shown.

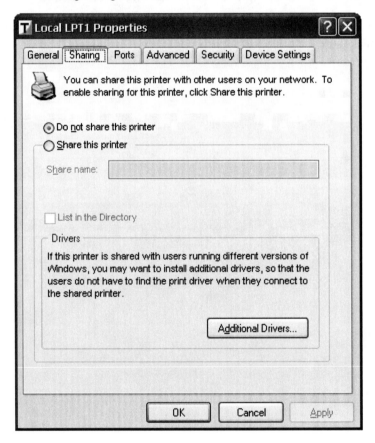

3. Select **Share this printer** and type the share name.

   What should you do if the printer is shared with computers that run different operating system versions?

   _____

4. Click **OK** to share the printer.

   How did the printer icon change?

   _____

7.5.10 ADD A NETWORK PRINTER (WIN2000/XP)

Scenario

You are configuring the printing environment for a Windows XP Professional computer. You want the workstation to be able to print to a network printer.

Your task in this lab is to use the Add Printer wizard to connect to the Dev-Prn1 printer on the NY-DEV-SRV1 network server.

Steps

Complete the following steps:

1. Click **Start/Printers and Faxes**.

2. In the Printer Tasks list, select the **Add a printer** task.

3. Click **Next** to begin the Add Printer wizard. The following dialog is shown:

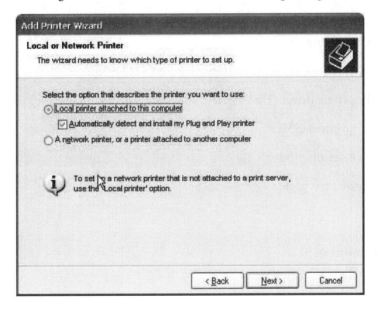

4. Select **A network printer, or a printer attached to another computer**. Click **Next**.

5. In the **Name** box, type the UNC path to the printer share. A UNC path uses the format *server_name\share_name*. Click **Next**.

6. Click **Finish**.

   How can you tell the difference between a network printer and a local printer?

   _____

7.5.11 CONFIGURE A NETWORK PRINTER (WIN98)

Scenario

You have just placed a new HP LaserJet IIISi print device in the R&D work area. It is connected to the UEC-SRV1 server. You want to set up the printer on your computer.

Your tasks are:

- Add a network printer.

- Browse the network to find the printer: UEC-SRV1\ HP3SI.

- Install the printer driver (HP LaserJet IIISi).

- Name this printer HP3Si.

- Make this a default printer.

- Do not print a test page.

Steps

Complete the following steps:

1. Click **Start/Settings/Printers**.

2. Double-click **Add Printer** to start the Add Printer Wizard.

3. Click **Next**.

4. Select **Network Printer**, then click **Next**.

5. Click the **Browse...** button. The following dialog is shown.

6. Expand the **UEC-SRV1** node and select **HP3SI**. Click **OK**.

7. Click **Next** to continue.

8. Select the printer manufacturer and model. Click **Next**.

9. Type **HP3Si** to change the printer name. Select **Yes** to make it the default printer, and click **Next**.

10. Click **No** when you are asked if you want to print a test page.

11. Click **Finish**.

7.6.5 PING A COMPUTER BY NAME (WIN98)

Scenario

Ping the computer named Ralph.

Steps

Complete the following steps:

1.   Click **Start/Programs/MS-DOS Prompt**.

2.   Type **ping ralph** and press Enter.

     What is the IP address for the computer?

     _____

     How many separate ping tests are performed?

     _____

7.6.6 USE PING (WINNT)

Scenario

You are a new user on the network and want to test your network connection using the PING command. The IP address of your computer is 142.111.2.16.

Do the following:

1. Enter the command that verifies the TCP/IP configuration of your computer.

2. Ping the IP address of Ralph, who is on a different subnet. His IP address is 142.111.3.11.

Steps

Complete the following steps:

1. Click the **Start/Programs/Command Prompt**.

2. Type **ipconfig**.

   Complete the following table with the information for this computer.

Parameter	Value
IP Address	
Subnet Mask	
Default Gateway	

3. To ping the remote device, type **ping 142.111.3.11**.

   Can this computer communicate with the remote computer?

   _____

4. To ping the remote device, type **ping 142.111.3.11**.

    Can this computer communicate with the remote computer?

    _____

5. Type **ipconfig /all**.

    Complete the following table with the information for this computer.

Parameter	Value
Host Name	
Physical Address	
DHCP Enabled	

    Note: If your DOS prompt window is too small, you can resize the window by pulling down the bottom of the window.

7.6.7 USE IPCONFIG AND PING TO TROUBLESHOOT

Scenario

You are a new user on the network and want to test your network connection using the PING command. You decide to use a systematic troubleshooting approach to testing network connectivity. The network diagram is shown below.

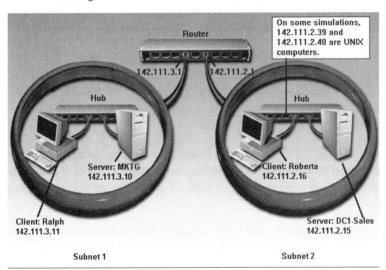

Do the following:

- Enter the command that verifies the TCP/IP configuration of your computer .

- Ping the loopback address.

- Ping your IP address (142.111.2.15).

- Ping your default gateway.

- Ping Ralph, who is on a different subnet. His IP address is 142.111.3.11.

Steps

Ping can be a powerful testing utility by allowing you to verify that TCP/IP is functioning at all the crucial points along a network, beginning with the workstation you're at. If ping fails to receive a response at any point along the network, you have isolated at least one problem spot. The following procedures point you to use ping as a testing tool.

- Ping the loopback address. Verify that TCP/IP has been installed and loaded properly by pinging the loopback address (127.0.0.1). When you ping the loopback address, your computer sends a packet down the TCP/IP protocol stack and back up.

- Ping your computer's IP address. Verify that TCP/IP is bound to your computer's adapter card correctly by pinging your computer's IP address (the **ipconfig /all** command reports the computer's IP address). When you ping your computer's IP address, your computer sends a packet on the wire and responds to that ping. This step does not work if TCP/IP is not bound to the network adapter card.

- Ping the default gateway. Check your connection to your default gateway by pinging its IP address (the **ipconfig /all** command reports the computer's default gateway). If the default gateway is incorrect, your computer may not be able to connect to remote networks.

- Ping a remote computer. Check your connection to a remote subnet by pinging a remote computer's (RALPH's) IP Address. If you cannot connect to the remote computer, try pinging the far side of the router. If this step is successful, then the connection problem is probably with the remote computer or the hardware between it and the router.

Before completing this lab, fill in the following table with the necessary commands to test the configuration and the network communication capabilities. As you work through the steps, fill in the results of each test.

Test	Command to Use	Result
View TCP/IP configuration information		
Ping the loopback address		Successful Unsuccessful
Ping the local address		Successful Unsuccessful
Ping the default gateway		Successful Unsuccessful
Ping the Ralph remote computer		Successful Unsuccessful

Complete the following steps:

1. Click the **Start/Programs/Command Prompt**.

2. Type **ipconfig**.

3. Ping the loopback address of the local computer.

   Note: If your DOS prompt window is too small, resize the window.

4. Ping the IP address of the local computer.

5. Ping the default gateway address.

6. Ping the Ralph computer.

   Note: The report for this lab will indicate that you performed the steps incorrectly if you performed them out of order. On a real system, you can perform these steps in any order.

7.6.8 TROUBLESHOOT TCP/IP 1

Scenario

You are working on Roberta's computer, which is assigned the IP address of 142.111.2.16. You are able to ping the IP address of the server (142.111.2.15) but you are unable to ping any other host. Find and fix the problem.

The network diagram is shown below.

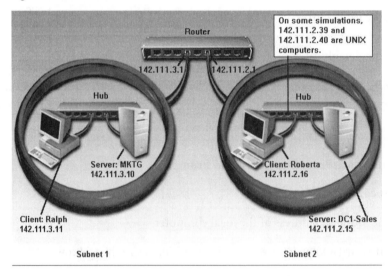

Steps

One of the first steps in troubleshooting TCP/IP communication problems is to verify the current configuration. Make sure the IP address, subnet mask, and default gateway values are correct. Complete the following table with the values that should be configured for this computer:

Parameter	Value
IP Address	
Subnet Mask	
Default Gateway	

Complete the following steps:

1. Click the **Start/Programs/Command Prompt**.

2. Type **ipconfig** to verify that TCP/IP has been initialized.

   What is the IP address of the computer?

   _____

   What is the problem?

   _____

3. Type **Exit** to close the command prompt window and press Enter.

4. To correct the problem, click **Start/Settings/Control Panel**.

5. Double-click the **Network** icon.

6. Click the **Protocols** tab.

7. Select **TCP/IP Protocol** in the list and click the **Properties...** button. The following dialog is shown:

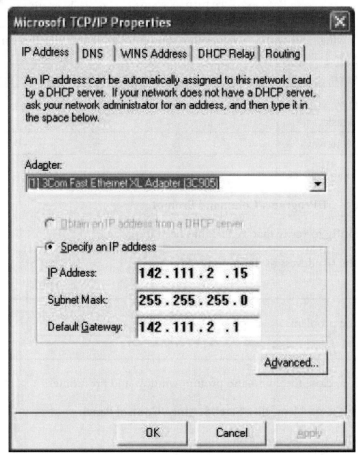

8. Change the IP address to **142.111.2.16**, then click **OK**.

9. Click **Close**.

10. To verify the configuration click the **Start/Programs/Command Prompt**.

11. Type **ipconfig**.

Complete the following table with the command you would use to test connectivity.

Test	Command to Use
Ping the loopback address	
Ping the local address	
Ping the default gateway	

Note: If your computer had restarted and tried to register the same IP address as the server, you would have received a duplicate IP error message. TCP/IP would not have initialized, and you would be unable to communicate over the network. You have to manually make the change.

7.6.9 TROUBLESHOOT TCP/IP 2

Scenario

You are working on Roberta's computer. You are unable to ping any remote hosts. Find and fix the problem.

The network diagram is shown below.

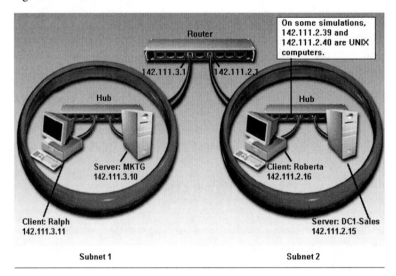

Steps

One of the first steps in troubleshooting TCP/IP communication problems is to verify the current configuration. Make sure the IP address, subnet mask, and default gateway values are correct. Complete the following table with the values that should be configured for this computer:

Parameter	Value
IP Address	
Subnet Mask	
Default Gateway	

Complete the following steps:

1. Click the **Start/Programs/Command Prompt**.

2. Type **ipconfig**.

   What configuration value is missing?

   _____

3. Type **Exit** to close the Command prompt and press Enter.

4. To correct the problem, right-click the **Network Neighborhood** icon and select **Properties**.

5. Click the **Protocols** tab.

6. Select **TCP/IP Protocol**, then click the **Properties...** button.

7. On the **IP Address** tab, modify the values as necessary to correct the problem. Click **OK**.

8. Click **Close**.

9. To verify that your solution solved the problem, click **Start/Programs/Command Prompt**.

10. Type **ipconfig**.

    What is the current value for the default gateway address?

    _____

11. Type **ping 142.111.2.1** to test the connection to the default gateway.

7.6.10 TROUBLESHOOT TCP/IP 3

Scenario

User Ralph has called and said that his computer is not able to access any remote hosts on the network. For this lab, you are at the user's computer. Find and fix the problem.

The network diagram is shown below.

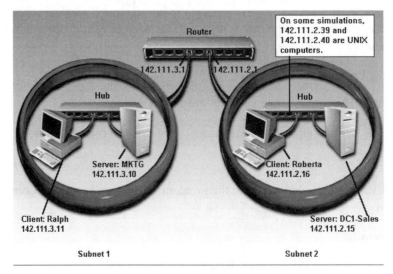

Steps

One of the first steps in troubleshooting TCP/IP communication problems is to verify the current configuration. Make sure the IP address, subnet mask, and default gateway values are correct. Complete the following table with the values that should be configured for this computer:

Parameter	Value
IP Address	
Subnet Mask	
Default Gateway	

Complete the following steps:

1. Click the **Start/Programs/Command Prompt.**

2. Type **ping 142.111.3.11** to test the connection to the computer's IP address

    What response did you receive?

    _____

3. Type **ipconfig.**

    What is Ralph's IP address as shown in ipconfig?

    _____

    Note: At this point, you should notice that you are unable to ping the computer's correct IP address of 142.111.3.11. This scenario would happen only if the user manually changed the IP address and then did not restart the computer. If there is a duplicate IP address on the network, the user will receive an error message after restarting.

4. Type **Exit** to close the Command prompt and press Enter.

5. To correct the computer's IP address, right-click **Network Neighborhood** and select **Properties.**

6. Click the **Protocols** tab.

7. Select **TCP/IP Protocol**, then click the **Properties...** button.

8. Change the IP address to **142.111.3.11**, then click **OK.**

9. Click **Close.**

10. To verify the change has corrected the problem, click **Start/Programs/Command Prompt.**

11. Type **ipconfig.**

8.0
Internet

8.1.3 CREATE A DIAL-UP INTERNET CONNECTION

Scenario

You are configuring network connections for a Windows XP Professional computer. You want to create a dial-up connection to the Internet on this computer.

Your task in this lab is to use the New Connection wizard in Network Connections to create a dial-up Internet connection on this computer manually with the following properties:

- Connection Name/ISP Name = Dial Internet

- Phone Number = 555-1234

- User Name = wacky123

- Password = 56passgo

- Always use this user name and password? = True

- Default Internet connection? = True

- Firewalled? = True

Steps

Complete the following steps:

1. Click **Start**, then right-click **My Network Places** and select **Properties**.

2. In the **Network Connections** folder, select the **Create a new connection** network task.

3. Click **Next** to start the New Connection wizard.

4. Verify **Connect to the Internet** is selected, then click **Next**.

5. Select **Set up my connection manually**, then click **Next**.

6. Verify **Connect using a dial-up modem** is selected and click **Next**.

7. Type **Dial Internet** as the ISP name (this will become the name of the network connection), then click **Next**.

8. Type **555-1234** as the phone number to dial. Click **Next**. The following dialog is shown:

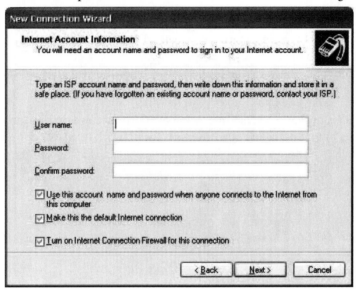

9. Populate the screen fields with the following required information.

   ○ User Name = wacky123

   ○ Password = 56passgo

   ○ Always use this user name and password? = True

   ○ Default Internet connection? = True

   ○ Firewalled? = True

   Click Next

10. Click **Finish**.

8.1.5 SHARE AN INTERNET CONNECTION

Scenario

You are configuring Internet connectivity for a small office network. You want all computers on the network to connect to the Internet using a shared dial-up network connection on a Windows XP Professional computer. You want the connection to be established automatically any time a computer tries to access the Internet.

Your task in this lab is to share the Dial Internet network connection on this computer. Allow on-demand dialing, but do not allow other users on the network to enable or disable the Internet connection manually.

Steps

Complete the following steps:

1. Click **Start**, then right-click **My Network Places** and select **Properties**.

2. Right-click a dial-up, VPN, or broadband connection and select **Properties**.

3. Click the **Advanced** tab. The following dialog is shown:

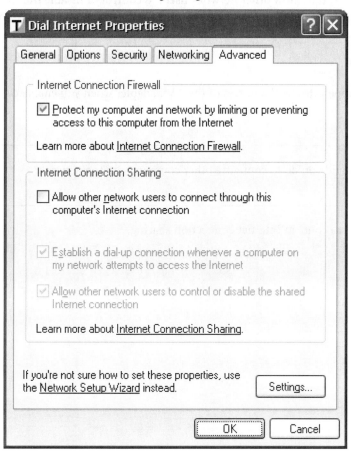

4. Select the **Allow other network users to connect through this computer's Internet connection** option.

   ◦ To enable on-demand dialing, which causes the connection to be established automatically when other users on the network need it, verify the **Establish a dial-up connection whenever a computer on my network attempts to access the Internet** option is selected.

   ◦ Deselect the **Allow other network users to control or disable the shared Internet connection** option to not let other users on the network enable (connect) or disable (disconnect) the shared connection manually.

   Click **OK**.

   What happens to the IP address of the LAN adapter when you enable connection sharing?

   _____

   What should you do to configure other computers on the network?

   _____

5. Click **Yes** to confirm Internet connection sharing.

8.2.1 CUSTOMIZE ADVANCED BROWSER SETTINGS

Scenario

You have just installed Windows XP Professional on your new computer at work. To complete the setup, you access a few web sites that have updated drivers for the hardware in your computer. As you do so, you realize that some of the browsing options are set differently than the browser on your old computer. You want to match the settings on your old computer with those on the new computer.

Edit the Advanced settings in Internet Options to enable the following settings:

- Show friendly URLs

- Show search results in the main window when searching from the Address bar

- Enable the Personalized Favorites Menu

Steps

Complete the following steps:

1. Click **Start/Control Panel.**

2. Click **Network and Internet Connections**.

3. Click **Internet Options**.

4. Click the **Advanced** tab. The following dialog is shown:

5. Enable the following settings under the **Browsing** heading:

    ○ **Enable Personalized Favorites Menu**

    ○ **Show friendly URLs**

6. Enable the following settings under the **Search from the Address bar** heading:

    ○ **Just display the results in the main window**

7. Click **OK**.

8.2.2 IMPROVE BROWSER PERFORMANCE

Scenario

You are using Windows XP on a Pentium II 300 with 128 MB of RAM and a 6-GB hard disk. You find that surfing the Internet is slow, even though you have a fast Internet connection. You want to increase browsing performance on your computer.

Improve browsing by:

- Disabling IE Automatic Update checking

- Disabling page transitions

- Disabling smooth scrolling

- Disabling animations, sounds, and videos in web pages

Steps

Complete the following steps:

1. Click **Start/Control Panel.**

2. Click **Network and Internet Connections.**

3. Click **Internet Options.**

4. Click the **Advanced** tab.

5. Disable the following settings under the **Browsing** heading:

   ○ **Automatically check for Internet Explorer updates**

   ○ **Enable page transitions**

   ○ **Use smooth scrolling**

6. Disable the following settings under the **Multimedia** heading:

   ○ ***Play animations in web pages**

   ○ ***Play sounds in web pages**

   ○ **Play videos in web pages**

7. Click **OK.**

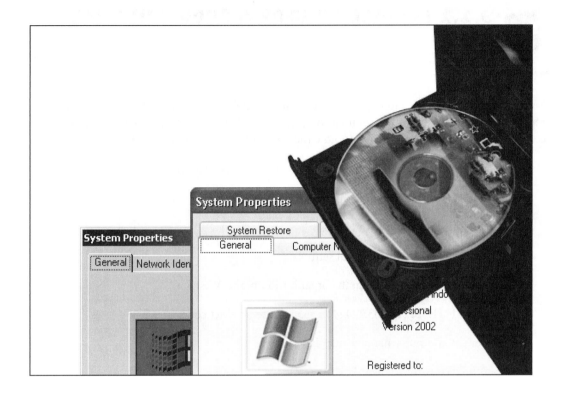

9.0

Installation, Configuration and Upgrade

9.1.1 INSTALL WINDOWS 2000 FOR DUAL BOOT

Scenario

Your company has decided to upgrade the operating system on the computers. Paula, a sales representative, has asked you to set up a computer for a dual boot. She has Windows 98 on her computer and wants to be able to boot to either Windows 98 or Windows 2000.

Based on her request, you will perform the following tasks in this simulation.

- Install Windows 2000 on the unpartitioned disk space.

- Format this partition with NTFS.

- Do not customize the regional settings.

- Enter the user name: Paula; the organization name: Westsim.

- Enter: 11111.22222.33333.44444.55555 as the product code.

- Enter the computer name: Paula_Drake.

- Set the password: password

- Set United States for the country and 801 for the area code.

- Enter 9 to dial out.

- Set the system date: December 1, 2001.

- Set the system time: 9:00:00 a.m, Mountain Time zone.

- Accept the Typical Settings on the Network Settings screen

- Make sure that this computer is a member of Domain1.

- Make sure that user must enter a user name and password to use this computer on the Users of this computer screen.

  Click the Done button after you finish the installation.

Note: In this simulation, the installation floppy disk is inserted for you.

Steps

Complete the following steps:

1. Select **No** when you are asked if you want to upgrade to Windows 2000.

2. Select **Install Windows 2000**.

    What happens if you choose to upgrade to Windows 2000?

    _____

3. Select **Install a new copy of Windows 2000 (Clean Install)**, then click **Next**.

4. Select **I don't accept this agreement**, then click **Next**.

    What message do you receive?

    _____

5. Click **Finish**.

6. Select **Install Windows 2000**.

7. Select **Install a new copy of Windows 2000 (Clean Install)**, then click **Next**.

8. Select **I accept this agreement**, then click **Next**.

9. Type **11111.22222.33333.44444.55555** as the product key and click **Next**.

    Which special option would you select to accommodate a user with hearing difficulty?

    _____

10. Click **Next**. The installation program runs through a series of steps which give you a command screen similar to the one shown here.

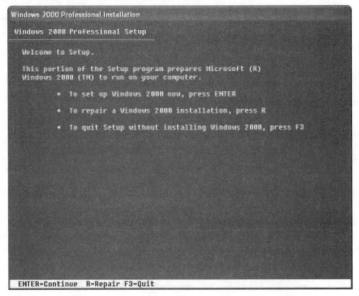

11. To continue the Windows 2000 setup, press the **Enter** key.

12. Use down arrow to select **Unpartitioned space** and press **Enter**.

13. Select **Format the Partition using the NTFS file system** and press **Enter**.

14. Click **Next** on Welcome to the Windows 2000 Setup Wizard screen.

15. Click **Next** on the Regional setting screen.

16. Type **Paula** as the user name and **Westsim** as the organization name, then click **Next**. The following dialog is shown:

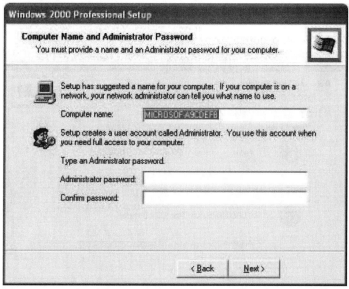

17. Type **Paula_Drake** as the computer name. Type **password** in the Administrator password box and Confirm password box and click **Next**. The following dialog is shown:

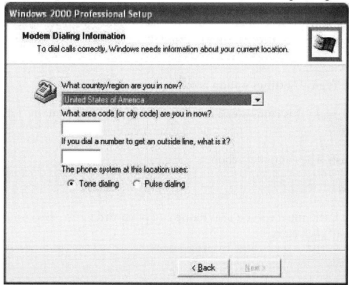

18. Verify the **United States of America** option is selected as the region on the Modem Dialing Information screen. Type **801** for the area code and **9** for the dial number for outside line, and then click **Next**.

The following dialog is shown:

19. Change the date to **December 1, 2001** on the Date and Time Setting screen. Change the time to **9:00:00 a.m.** Select **Mountain Time (US & Canada)** for the time zone and click **Next**.

20. Verify the **Typical Settings** option is selected and click **Next**.

21. Select **Yes, make this computer a member of the following domain**: Type **Domain1** and click **Next**.

22. Click **Finish**. The computer reboots.

23. Click **Next**.

24. Verify the **Users must enter a user name and password to use this computer** option is selected and click **Next**.

25. Click **Finish**.

9.2.2 INSTALL WINDOWS 2000 FROM CD-ROM

Scenario

You have just bought a computer with 8 GB of hard disk space and no operating system installed. You want to install Windows 2000 operating system on this computer.

Your tasks in this simulation are:

- Create a 2000 Mb partition and leave the rest of the disk unpartitioned.

- Format the partition with the NTFS file system.

- Do not customize the Regional Settings.

- Enter whatever name you want for the user name and or organization name.

- Enter 12345.FFFFF.54321.DDDDD.TTTTT as the product key.

- Name the computer Workstation2

- Set the password to study

- Select United States of America for the country.

- Enter your area code.

- Set the system date to March 5, 2002

- Set the system time to 8:30.00 a.m.

- Select your time zone.

- Select Typical for the setup.

- Make sure that the user must enter the user name and password to use the computer.

Click the Done button after you finish the installation.

Note: In this simulation, the installation floppy disk is inserted for you.

Steps

The first installation floppy disk has already been inserted in A drive. When you click Continue after reading the scenario, the installation starts.

Complete the following steps:

1. Press **Enter** when you are asked to insert Setup Disk 2, Disk 3 and Disk 4.

2. Press **Enter** to accept the option **To set up Windows 2000 now**.

3. Press **F8** to accept the Microsoft user license agreement.

4. Press **C** to partition the disk.

5. Press **backspace** to delete the assigned partition size, type **2000** for new partition size and press **Enter**.

6. Highlight the **C: New (Unformatted)** partition and press **Enter** to set up Windows 2000.

7. Select **Format the Partition using the NTFS file system option** and press **Enter**.

8. Click **Next** to continue on the Welcome to the Windows 2000 Setup Wizard.

9. Click **Next** on the Regional Settings screen to continue.

10. Type your **name** and your **company name**, then click **Next**.

11. Type **12345.FFFFF.54321.DDDDD.TTTTT** in the Product Key box and click **Next**.

12. Type **Workstation2** as the computer name.

13. Type **study** as the Administrator password and Confirm the password, then click **Next**.

14. Select **United States of America** as the region. Type **your own area code** and click **Next**.

15. Change the date to **March 5, 2002** on the Date and Time Setting screen. Change the time to **8:30.00 a.m.** Select **your own time zone** and click **Next**.

16. Verify the **Typical Settings** option is selected and click **Next**.

17. Select **Yes, make this computer a member of the following domain:** option. Type **Portland** as the domain name and click **Next**.

18. Click **Finish**. Now the computer reboots itself.

19. Click **Next**.

20. Select **Users must enter a user name and password to use this computer** and click **Next**.

21. Click **Finish**.

9.2.3 INSTALL WINDOWS 2000 WITH BOOT FLOPPIES

Scenario

A client has asked you to set up a Windows 2000 computer for her.

Based on her request, you will perform the following tasks in this simulation.

1. Set up Windows 2000 on the unpartitioned disk and let the installation automatically format the disk.

2. Select NTFS for the file system.

3. Do not customize the regional setting

4. Enter the user name: Elaine Smith, leave the organization name blank.

5. Enter: W2CCC.123AA.456BB.789DD.EEEEE as the product code.

6. Name the computer: Home_Office

7. Set the password: elainesmith

8. On the Modem dialing Information screen, select United States for the country, area code: 207.

9. Set the system date: December 10, 2001.

10. Set the system time: 10:00:00 a.m.

11. Select Eastern Time for Time Zone

12. Select Typical Settings on the Network Settings screen

13. Select No this computer is not on the network on the Workgroup and Computer Domain screen.

14. Select User must enter a user name and password to use this computer on the Users of this computer screen.

    Click the Done button after you finish the installation.

Note: In this simulation, the installation floppy disk is inserted for you.

Steps

The first installation floppy disk has already been inserted in A drive. When you click Continue after reading the scenario, the installation starts.

Complete the following steps:

1. Press **Enter** when you are asked to insert Setup Disk 2, Disk 3 and Disk 4.

2. Press **Enter** to **Set up Windows 2000 now** on the Windows 2000 Professional Setup screen.

3. Press **F8** to accept the Microsoft user license agreement.

4. Press **Enter** to set up Windows 2000 on the unpartitioned space.

5. Select **Format the Partition using NTFS file system**. Press **Enter** to let the setup program format the C drive.

6. Click **Next**.

7. Click **Next** on the Regional Settings screen.

8. Type **Elaine Smith** as the Name and leave the Organization text box blank, then click **Next**.

9. Type **W2CCC-123AA-456BB-789DD-EEEEE** in the product key box and click **Next**.

10. Type **Home_Office** in the computer name text box. Type **elainesmith** in the administrator password box and confirm the password. Click **Next**.

11. Verify the **United States of America** option is the region on the Modem Dialing Information screen. Type **207** for the area code and click **Next**.

12. Change the date to **December 10, 2001**. Change the time to **10:00:00 a.m.** Select **Eastern Time** for the time zone and click **Next**.

13. Verify the **Typical Settings** option is selected and click **Next**.

14. Select **No, this computer is not on the network.....** option click **Next**.

15. Click **Finish**. Now the computer reboots.

16. Click **Next** on the Welcome to the Network Identification Wizard screen.

17. Select **Users must enter a user name and password to use this computer** and click **Next**.

18. Click **Finish**.

9.3.1 DELETE AND CREATE PARTITIONS FOR DUAL BOOT

Scenario

You have a Windows 95 computer with one primary partition and one extended partition which has two logical drives. You decide to make two primary partitions out of the 8 GB of disk space so that you can install Windows 98 and Windows 2000 operating systems for dual boot.

You have already booted the computer with a Win98 boot floppy that contains FDISK.EXE.

Your tasks:

1. Delete the existing partitions.

2. Partition the disk with one primary partition with half of the disk space. Leave the other half of the disk space unpartitioned for dual boot.

3. Make the primary partition the active partition.

Note: You have already booted the computer with a Win98 boot floppy that contains FDISK.EXE and can start your partitioning now.

Steps

Boot the computer with a boot floppy that contains FDISK.EXE (we assume that this step has been done for this simulation).

Complete the following steps:

1. Type **FDISK** and press Enter.

2. Verify **Y** is selected and press Enter.

3. Type **3** to select Delete partition or Logical DOS Drive, then press Enter.

4. Type **3** to select Delete Logical DOS Drive(s) in the Extended DOS Partition, then press Enter.

    What drives currently make up the extended DOS partition?

    _____

5. Type **D** to delete D drive and press Enter.

6. Type **D** for the D drive volume label and press Enter.

7. Type **Y** and press Enter.

    How has the extended of extended DOS partition changed?

    _____

8. Type **E** to delete E drive and press Enter.

9. Type **E** and press Enter.

10. Type **Y** and press Enter.

11. Press Esc.

12. Type **3** to select Delete partition or Logical DOS Drive, then press Enter.

13. Type **2** to select Delete Extended DOS partition, then press Enter.

    How many partitions are listed in the partition table?

    _____

14. Type **Y** and press Enter. The following dialog is shown:

```
Dos

                    Delete Extended DOS Partition
Current fixed disk drive: 1

Partition  Status   Type    Volume Label  Mbytes   System    Usage
  C: 1       A    PRI DOS      WIN95      4000     UNKNOWN    48%


Total disk space is 8192 Mbytes (1 Mbyte = 1048576 bytes)
WARNING! Data in the deleted Extended DOS Partition will be lost.



Extended DOS Partition deleted

Press Esc to continue|
```

How many partitions are listed in the partition table?

_____

15. Press Esc.

16. Type **3** to select Delete partition or Logical DOS Drive, then press Enter.

17. Select option **1. Delete Primary DOS Partition**, then press Enter.

18. Accept **1** as the primary partition to delete and press Enter.

19. Type **Win95** as the Volume Label and press Enter.

20. Type **Y** and press Enter.

21. Press Esc.

22. Accept option **1. Create DOS partition or Logical DOS Drive, then** press Enter.

23. Accept option **1. Create Primary DOS Partition, then** press Enter.

24. Type **N** and press Enter. The following dialog is shown:

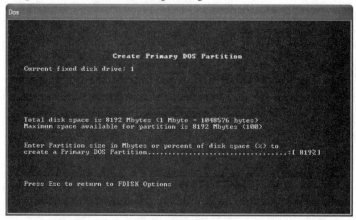

25. Press the Backspace key to empty the box and type **50%,** then press Enter.

26. The information on the screen informs you that the primary DOS partition has been created. Press Esc.

27. Type **2** to select Set active partition and press Enter.

28. Type **1** and press Enter.

29. Press Esc and Esc.

30. Press Esc again.